April 2021

There are a few of us old, retired officers who are equally sick of the lack of humanity plaguing our former profession - and I happen to be one of them. Use as you see fit, and let's get this done, once and for all.

B M

RISE OF THE OATHBREAKERS

D. B. McCrea

To the Martians on the Moon of Glencoe;

Cousin Chad, one of the good guys;

to K and J;

and One More, who served as my inspiration.

An officer has just returned home from a late-night patrol and has yet to step from his patrol vehicle. Within sight of the officer (to the front right) is a closed "mom and pop" shop, which will not reopen for several hours. The shop is located less than one-half block away on the corner of "bar row". One-half block to the officer's right is Casey's convenience store, likewise scheduled to reopen in a few hours.

From inside the darkened cab of the patrol vehicle, the officer sees two quick, somewhat diffuse, flashes of light and realizes someone is parked out of view on the far side of the convenience store. His interest piqued, the officer watches and waits, curious as to why, at 2:20 in the morning, someone would twice flash the headlights in the general direction of the mom and pop shop?

After several minutes the headlights come on. The driver quickly crosses the street and parks in front of the shop. Seconds later, a darkened silhouette emerges from a side door and runs to the car. The pair take off headed to an unknown destination.

Based upon the facts and circumstances presented above, do you believe the officer has "reasonable suspicion" to justify stopping and detaining the driver and passenger to conduct a brief investigation?

If so, why, and under what specific authority?

THE MEASURE OF A MAN IS WHAT HE DOES WITH POWER.

- PLATO -

WHO WILL HOLD THE POLICE ACCOUNT-
ABLE, IF NOT FOR THE CITIZENS?

- D.B. McCREA -

Shown are three officers from the Sioux Falls, South Dakota Police Department. The officers first tackled, then arrested, an American citizen who chose a public sidewalk as the platform to exercise his right of free speech under the First Amendment to the United States Constitution. Extending one's middle finger and yelling "[Expletive] the police!" may be in poor taste; however, they are not against the law √ (**State of South Dakota v. Suhn 2008**). Citizens have the right to be critical of the government, even if the criticism is comprised of a rude gesture and an unflattering salutation.

Amendment I

Congress shall make no law respecting an establishment of religion, or prohibiting the free exercise thereof; or abridging the freedom of speech, or of the press; or the right of the people peaceably to assemble, and to petition the government for a redress of grievances.

Amendment II

A well regulated Militia, being necessary to the security of a free State, the right of the people to keep and bear Arms shall not be infringed.

Amendment IV

The right of the people to be secure in their persons, houses, papers, and effects, against unreasonable searches and seizures, shall not be violated, and no warrants shall issue, but upon probable cause, supported by oath or affirmation, and particularly describing the place to be searched, and the persons or things to be seized (author: without any one of these three amendments, the whole of the Constitution would simply collapse).

Deprivation of Rights Under Color of Law
√ **Title 18, U.S.C., Section 242,** makes it a crime for a person acting under color of any law to willfully deprive a person of a right or privilege protected by the Constitution or laws of the United States.

Giglio Impairment
√ **(Giglio v. United States 1972).** An officer who is "Giglio impaired" is one whose testimonial integrity has been "impeached", or successfully called into question by defense counsel. Under Giglio, an officer with a documented history of professional dishonesty - such as lying to a supervisor - can be excluded from testifying at trial. (In Baltimore, for example, there are 53 police officers currently disallowed from testifying.)

The "Katz Test"
√ **Katz v. United States, 389 U.S. 347 (1967),** was a landmark decision of the U.S. Supreme Court in which the Court redefined what constitutes "searches" and "seizures" with regard to the protections of the Fourth Amendment to the U.S. Constitution. It extended Fourth

Amendment protection beyond the traditional confines of citizens' homes and property, and a concurring opinion filed by Justice John Marshall Harlan II set forth what is now known as the "Katz test" that inquires whether a person in a certain circumstance has a "reasonable expectation of privacy" against intrusion by government or law enforcement. The Katz test has been used in thousands of cases, particularly with the advancement of technology that poses new questions on expectations of privacy.

In layman's terms, the Katz test is comprised of two essential elements: does a person have an expectation of privacy in a given area; and is that expectation of privacy *reasonable*. Its significance cannot be overstated as the Katz test is foundational to legal decisions affecting searches and seizures of persons or property under the Fourth Amendment.

√ Graham v. Connor (1989) and the "Test of Objective Reasonableness"

In any use of force review, courts will apply the three "Graham Factors" - without the benefit of 20/20 hindsight - to determine if the use of force is justified (not an exhaustive list):

1) the severity of the crime at issue

2) whether the suspect poses an immediate threat to the safety of the officers or others

3) whether the suspect is actively resisting arrest or attempting to resist arrest

Standards of Proof - on a scale from 0 to 100%
Reasonable Suspicion of a Crime: (minimum standard to detain)...25%
Probable Cause: (minimum standard to arrest)...51%
A Preponderance of the Evidence: (civil standard)...51%
Clear and Convincing...70%
Beyond a Reasonable Doubt: (minimum criminal standard to convict)...95%

Reasonable Suspicion* - a set of articulable facts and circumstances that would lead a reasonable person to believe that a specific crime has been committed, is being committed, or is about to be committed by a particular person. Reasonable suspicion of a crime cannot be based upon a hunch, gut feeling, or simply to conduct a "fishing expedition". Reasonable suspicion falls short of probable cause to search, ticket, or arrest; however, it gives the officer the lawful authority to stop and briefly detain, as well as identify the person. **NOTE:** Affording police officers the latitude to define what is "reasonable suspicion", without also articulating a particular crime, means an end to liberty and the inevitable growth of the police state. This will be covered extensively throughout the book. It is that important.

A cursory pat-down for weapons is authorized only after the officer has cleared two legal hurdles: 1) at a minimum, the person is lawfully detained under reasonable suspicion of a particular crime, and 2) IF THE OFFICER CAN CLEARLY ARTICULATE WHY THEY BELIEVE THE PERSON MAY BE ARMED AND DANGEROUS. A pat-down cannot be done simply as a matter of routine.

Probable Cause - a set of articulable facts and circumstances that would lead a reasonable person to believe that 1) a particular crime has been committed, and 2) a particular person or persons committed the crime.

The three types of police-citizen encounters:
1. Consensual or voluntary, where either party can walk away
2. Investigative detention, based on reasonable suspicion
3. Arrest, based on probable cause

*In addition to other applicable case law such as √ **(Terry v. Ohio 1968)**, courts have ruled in √ **U.S. v. Slocumb (4th Cir. 2015)** and √ **U.S. v. Monsivais (5th Cir. 2017)** that mere suspicion alone does <u>not</u> rise to reasonable suspicion of a crime.

Six Common Errors*

Six common errors a police officer makes leading to an unconstitutional stop and subsequent detention are:

- Detaining based upon mere suspicion alone

- Detaining because the officer received a call for service, without reasonable suspicion of a crime

- Detaining because the officer or reporting party simply did not like what the person was doing, even though the activity was lawful

- Detaining based upon a hunch, gut feeling, or simply to conduct a "fishing expedition"

- Detaining, hoping to find a reason to detain (i.e. "You're detained until we can figure out what's going on") without reasonable suspicion of a crime

- Detaining based solely on a "happenstance of geography", in which a person happens to occupy an area with a known history of criminal activity

None of the six rises to the level of reasonable suspicion of a crime, thereby justifying a detention. Yet officers will use any one of the six as an excuse to violate a person's constitutional rights.

*Officers will claim that they have the "right" to do something while in the performance of their duties. This is categorically false. Only the citizens have rights guaranteed under the Constitution. Law enforcement officers have <u>authority</u> but nothing more. Never allow a law enforcement officer to conflate their authority with the rights of citizens; rights trump authority, every time!

When dealing with the police, regardless of the circumstances, it is important to remember these tips:

* Keep your hands on the steering wheel and your hands out of your pockets

* Make no sudden movement, one that can be deemed "furtive"

* Avoid an argument. More often than not the officer is right

* Follow the officer's instructions, within reason of course

* Ask for the officer's name and badge number

* Do not volunteer too much information

* Be an adult, even if the officer is not

* Record encounters with the police

* Avoid confrontation, generally

* NEVER consent to a search

* NEVER resist an arrest

* Fight injustice in the courtroom, NEVER IN THE STREET

* Most importantly, KNOW YOUR RIGHTS

DISCLAIMER AND BACKGROUND

OATHBREAKER. NOUN. (PLURAL OATHBREAKERS) A
member of the political ruling class, police force, or military
who takes an oath to support and defend the Constitution
of the United States, but subsequently acts based upon
personal opinion or whatever is in their best interest.
One who is subject to contrivance and lack of candor.

As the title suggests, "Rise of the Oathbreakers" is more
than a book about some of my more memorable encounters with
the sporting public. Where the book strays from the conventional is
through the presentation of an honest, no-holds-barred assessment
of the current state of law enforcement in America. Especially, but
not exclusively, in the aftermath of the 9/11 terrorist attacks. It will
further address the sensitive issue of racism in law enforcement; as
well as the importance of restoring a fundamental sense of humanity
to a profession that has clearly lost its way.

Like the saying "vote early, vote often" that characterizes
chronic corruption in the Chicago-area political machine, some
police officers (i.e. the "oathbreakers") will subvert the constitutional
rights of citizens early and often.

In general terms, these subversions include unconstitutional searches and seizures; illegal detentions and arrests; manufacturing crimes; applying unreasonable or excessive force; acting outside the scope of their lawful authority; and bullying citizens into surrendering their rights by citing phantom officer safety concerns. Each of these will be discussed to a varying degree.

Under no circumstance should the book be interpreted as a "call to arms" against any entity of law enforcement, neither individually nor collectively - although I admit my critique is extremely harsh at times. Despite the many serious issues plaguing law enforcement today, I would never do something so unconscionable to my sisters and brothers with whom I shared a badge for 23 years.

My critique of police actions is comprised of three main parts, each with relatively equal value: facts, generalizations based upon informed opinion, and practical experience. It is an honest assessment if nothing else. Understand that the interpretation of legal matters discussed in the book neither begins nor ends with me. Frankly, I could be wrong on some issues. Test my conclusions for yourself! Furthermore, be sure to seek the legal advice of a qualified attorney on matters involving the law. This cannot be stressed enough.

Law enforcement and its many attached legal issues are topics that hardly remain static. This results in widespread inconsistencies, even between the eleven independent Circuit Courts of Appeals √ (ex. **Turner v. Driver 5th Cir. 2017**). A legal decision rendered in one Circuit may not necessarily be recognized in another; only as a legal precedent, typically.

Anecdotal stories of police misconduct were chosen for their relevance to a particular topic. This was quite a chore given the number of online videos to choose from. My sincerest thanks to "First

Amendment Auditors" and "Cop Watchers" ("activists", collectively) who film their encounters with the police and make them available to watch on YouTube. This book would not have been possible without their hard work and willingness to take a stand against government-sponsored tyranny.

It is not uncommon for an oathbreaker to falsely arrest an activist and violate one or more of their constitutional rights while doing so. Unfortunately, not having access to the official court records made it difficult to learn, with any degree of certainty, whether a resulting civil rights lawsuit was resolved in favor of the activist. Seeing that we live in the age of the Internet, an independent search using the name of the activist, involved officer, and/or agency may yield the results.

Used liberally throughout the book are reductio ad absurdum arguments, or "Arguments of Absurdity". These are meant to expose the most common logical fallacies inherent with today's policing and, furthermore, to showcase just how ridiculous these fallacies appear when viewed from an extreme perspective.

Minor redundancies appear from time to time, primarily where oathbreakers parlay mere suspicion into an unconstitutional detention and subsequently issue a unilateral "Show me ID or else!" ultimatum. Although I have tried to limit these redundancies, it was unavoidable given the overlapping subject matter.

To quell any concerns about the use of profanity, prospective readers have my assurance that not one word appears in the book. Scout's honor! An acceptable literary compromise was to use either [expletive] or an [*] in its place.

Unrelated to the use of profanity is the term "simple-minded supervisors" found in Chapter 25. It is used to better describe three former simple-minded supervisors, each of whom I found quite disagreeable. No disrespect is intended, either real or implied, to anyone except the three simple-minded supervisors.

> Pay attention, oathbreakers. I want you to know that this is your book. It was written because of you.

Pay attention, oathbreakers. I want you to know that this is your book. It was written because of you. It should not have been necessary until it became necessary. The onus is on you to clean up your act. To make amends with the people you have falsely arrested or callously disrespected. To make it right with the people whose lives you have ruined.

Why do you believe chains and a cage is the solution to every problem? Answer the question! We are not animals. We are not your property. We are human beings; yet we find ourselves looking at you through steel bars, sometimes unjustly, as if we were monkeys at the zoo. You toss us peanuts and laugh along with the zookeepers. How dare you!

You owe us your allegiance. We do not owe you ours. Respect us and we will try to respect you in return. Stop hurting us, just because you can. Stop killing us, just because you said, "I feared for my life!" Like three of you did when you gunned down 35-year-old Ricardo Diaz-Zeferino in Gardena, California. Like one of you did when he shot and killed the beautiful 28-year-old Atatiana Jefferson in Fort Worth, Texas. They lie buried, while you still roam the earth.

Stop, before you cross the Rubicon. Work with the community. Get to know the people you serve. At least make the effort. Fake it if need be. Just try.

CHAPTER ONE

Honest Introspection

A police officer is a guardian by nature and a warrior when
necessary. They are expected to know the difference.

A question commonly asked, with good reason, is "Why
do police officers so often fail to intervene when they witness another
officer bullying a person and violating their constitutional rights?"
What follows is not to excuse the non-interventionist behavior of
some police officers, only my best attempt to explain it.

Broadly speaking, there are two types of personalities: "alpha"
and "beta". An officer with an "alpha" personality is typically more
aggressive and confrontational. An officer with a "beta" personality
is just the opposite, preferring to avoid confrontation by not starting
a confrontation. Alphas will escalate a contact for no reason other
than they WANT to escalate, whereas betas will escalate only when
they NEED to escalate. **NOTE:** Because of an alpha's predilection to
escalate every contact, those who choose to assert their constitutional

rights during police interactions should do so prudently, without unnecessary fanfare or drama. It is far better to handle an alpha with knowledge than it is with malice.

From top to bottom, alphas dominate the law enforcement profession. This is to be expected since alphas are more likely to choose law enforcement as a career and more likely to seek in-house promotions. Alphas hire mostly alphas, train mostly alphas, and supervise mostly alphas. What could possibly go wrong? Plenty!

In nearly every instance in which an officer fails to intervene, it is because the officer lacks the desire to intervene. Lacking the desire to intervene has nothing to do with laziness or hesitant benevolence. These officers WANT to go hands-on and are simply waiting for the right opportunity to join the fray.

It is a typical playground maneuver where the officer-in-waiting can invoke plausible deniability by asserting his role was secondary to that of the instigator: "Yeah, I kicked the kid in the head, but 'instigator Timmy' kicked the kid in the head first!"

Conversely, there are officers who want to intervene but choose not to, either because the instigator is of higher rank or the instigator is too well-connected within the agency or police union. This is a byproduct of police culture where testosterone and swagger carry the day. "Breaking ranks" is heresy - and the punishment is swift.

Excepting a most egregious example, my hesitation to intervene was knowing in advance that the supervisors - either by an act of omission or commission - would band together to protect one of their own (numerous examples can be found in Chapter 25). This mindset ran from the field to the Pierre headquarters, sometimes reaching the level of the Governor's Office.

By and large, the bosses were untouchable, as were their fair-haired subordinate officers. Other than keeping a watchful eye, there was nothing I could say or do to change the status quo. Doing what was legal and proper had fallen out of favor with upper-level management.

The relatively few betas who enter the profession can soon become overwhelmed by the incredibly hostile and highly-dysfunctional work environment created by alphas. It is a repressive - often brutal - system of internal governance; fraught with conflict and fueled by managerial incompetence. To survive in such a toxic environment, betas tend to adopt a "bunker mentality"; which is necessary to keep both their job and their sanity. Trust me, alphas will always find a way to screw with betas.

German philosopher, Friedrich Nietzsche, wrote in 1882, "In individuals, insanity is rare; but in groups...it is the rule." Nietzsche could have been writing about law enforcement in the modern era, in what some would undoubtedly believe was a largely self-inflicted descent into indiscriminate madness. Nietzsche himself went mad, which, to me at least, would make him a subject-matter expert.

> ...how well a contact starts often determines how well a contact ends.

Far too many officers fail to appreciate the importance of making a good first impression; meaning, how well a contact starts often determines how well a contact ends. An officer who needs to be reminded of this is clearly headed in the wrong direction. What is worse is needing to remind field supervisors and upper-level management as well.

As an officer, my most effective "weapon" had little to do with what I was carrying on my gun belt. Alphas make the mistake of thinking their load-bearing vest - weighted down with 20mm Oerlikon rounds and a half dozen bite-size Hellfire missiles - is what keeps them alive on the street. What kept me alive was good training, excellent equipment, and treating others as human beings. There are no other possible explanations, not even one.

New officers are still being trained to believe that politeness is a weakness and that every person they contact, regardless of the circumstances, is either Darth Vader or Jack the Ripper. Not true. The vast majority of people would never dream of hurting an officer. Looking at others as a potential threat is fine; however, looking at others as an actual threat is not. Acting "preemptively" can backfire on an officer by creating a problem when before there were none.

> ...looking at others as a potential threat is fine; however, looking at others as an actual threat is not.

Moreover, believing that politeness is a weakness is hopelessly counterintuitive because it suggests two things: being polite impairs officer safety - it does not! - and being a jerk is a better alternative. An important reminder to officers is that situational awareness is best maintained by level-headedness. Neither should aggressiveness be used in lieu of assertiveness, the former used only when necessary.

Something else that alphas seldom grasp is how quickly a gruff demeanor on their part can set someone off, especially those who are already walking a fine line between being cooperative and uncooperative. This is how contacts escalate. Stir in an alpha's massive ego and I dare anyone to convince me that this is a more effective form of communication.

Regarding new officers, it is my sincerest hope that they would pledge to never lose sight of their humanity; that they would strive to hold themselves to a level of personal and professional accountability greater than the citizens they serve.

This "accountability pledge" is not intended to usurp the pledge that new officers take to uphold and defend the Constitution; but rather, as a supplemental pledge. Officers who place humanity first are less likely to overstep their authority and more likely to build trust within the community. This is an attainable goal, certainly one worth striving for.

If oathbreakers were to engage in honest introspection, they might learn that it is they who are the problem, not the people they serve. Moreover, being a police officer is not a form of indentured servitude. Either do it right or do something else for a living, please and thank you!

Perhaps it would further the cause if oathbreakers were to look at things from a slightly different perspective, one beginning and ending with just one question: "Would you want your family members to be treated the same way that you treat the family members of others?" It is not a trick question, or is that too much to ask of an oathbreaker?

Several decades ago, there was a young and inexperienced game warden who lamented how he had checked just one hunter while on evening patrol. "I might as well have stayed home!" the rookie complained. "That's the wrong way to look at it," said the wizened old warden who overheard the remark. "You checked more like five hunters because the hunter went home and told four of his buddies that he'd been checked by a game warden."

That was over thirty-five years ago, yet I remember it vividly to this day. Treat one hunter poorly and earn five potential enemies, or treat one hunter well and earn five potential friends. My colleague was talking about the "Golden Rule", only slightly modified to fit a game warden narrative.

Police officers will talk about power and authority as it relates only to themselves. True power and authority are derived from the heart and are best used to make a difference in someone else's life, one that does not always involve chains and a cage.

There was another piece of advice that the wizened old warden shared with me that night. "That's how you change the world, you know," he said earnestly. "It's done one person at a time."

I remember it vividly to this day, too.

CHAPTER TWO

What's a Fail-Safe?

meaning, definition, explanation...

"Vicarious liability" has legal roots dating back to slav-ery and the passage of the Civil Rights Act of 1871 (42 U.S.C. § 1983). Simply put, the Act of 1871 allows people to sue the government for civil rights violations. It mainly affects the law enforcement profession, since it is they who continue to be the primary purveyor of constitutional injustices. "Vicarious liability", as it relates to law enforcement, has been broken into three general categories: (negligent) hiring, training, and retention.

Negligent hiring is self-explanatory, in that it requires an enforcement agency to hire the "right" kind of officer versus hiring the "wrong" kind of officer. Agencies have available to them a wide variety of tools to cull the herd of prospective candidates. These include exhaustive background checks; multiple one-on-one interviews (including friends, family, and previous employers); written examinations; lie detector tests; and psychological evaluations.

Although negligent training is largely self-explanatory, the same may not be true for negligent retention. Negligent retention occurs when an agency keeps an officer on the street despite a documented history of misconduct. Agencies that fail to properly investigate a report of officer misconduct are signaling (to the officer) their tacit approval to engage in further misconduct. It is this perceived lack of internal oversight that has given rise to the present-day understanding of the "thin blue line".

Throughout its history, the "thin blue line" was seen as police officers acting as a bulwark between civilized society and civil unrest. For more and more citizens, the term has acquired a much different meaning. By civilian standards, the thin blue line is seen as a rigged system of jurisprudence whereby police officers have been granted the autonomy to police themselves. What began as a system of supposed checks and balances has become a system wherein too little is checked and even less is balanced.

> One of the greatest impediments to holding police officers accountable for alleged misconduct - other than agency negligence - are the police unions.

One of the greatest impediments to holding police officers accountable for alleged misconduct - other than agency negligence - are the police unions. Joe Gamaldi, President of the Houston, Texas Police Officers Union, spoke frightening words about WE THE PEOPLE during a January 28, 2019 press conference. His remarks came just three days after five Houston police officers were shot and wounded during service of a drug-related search warrant at a private residence in Houston.

Denver Police Officer Shawn Miller racked up forty complaints in ten years, many of which were complaints of excessive force. Virtually all went unpunished.

Gamaldi's scathing indictment of critics of the police - "dirtbags" according to Gamaldi - was predictable, yet incorrectly placed.

Two of the officers involved with the botched raid, Gerald Goines and Steven Bryant, would eventually be charged with two counts of murder and tampering with evidence, respectively. Goines lied on the search warrant affidavit, while Bryant lied on an after-action report.

It was seven months after the murders of Rhogena Nicholas and Dennis Tuttle before Union President Gamaldi announced that the union would no longer pay Gerald Goines' legal fees. It was a different story for Steven Bryant. "His legal expenses will be taken care of until the very end" according to one union official.

On August 16, 2019, Joe Gamaldi was elected National Vice President of the Fraternal Order of Police (FOP). Two years earlier, FOP members had petitioned the federal government to reverse its ban on racial profiling. Ray Hunt, Gamaldi's police union predecessor in Houston, said officers responded to Gamaldi because of his energy and passion for police officers' 'rights'.

A police union's undying support for one of its members, regardless of the circumstances, is on its face the very definition of police corruption. It is just one of the reasons why much of the public have come to view law enforcement with a jaundiced eye; why more and more citizens have grown weary of the homage officers pay to the thin blue line and its inherent divisiveness.

Officers have sewn onto their uniforms, and plastered onto the sides of their patrol vehicles, a prominent thin blue line flag; a desecration of the American flag, tinged with a menacing shade of black and accented with a gaudy blue line running horizontally through the middle. It is a disturbing rendition of the flag that once flew with such dignity and honor atop Iwo Jima's Mt. Suribachi during WWII. Some see it as signaling membership in a street gang, the same way that the Crips and the Bloods signal membership in their gangs by the colors blue and red, respectively.

Designed to hold the thin blue line in check is a bottom-to-top network of "fail-safes". "Fail-safes" are meant to be the first, or last, line of defense against a catastrophic failure; such as the ability to recall a nuclear bomber en route to a target. Accordingly, the first fail-safe put in place to safeguard citizens from a dirtbag cop like Joe Gamaldi is the police officer "<u>prospect</u>".

Norman

No civilian is forced into law enforcement, any more than a civilian is forced to join the military. A "prospect" must approach the agency voluntarily and ask to be hired. "Trust me!" is the promise a prospect makes to the community the moment they send in an application for employment. "Trust me? Heck no!" is the promise a prospect might be making if police misconduct is as pervasive as it appears.

Next in line is the <u>agency</u>, which is legally obligated not to hand a badge and a gun to someone like Norman Bates, the misogynistic serial killer from Sir Alfred Hitchcock's appropriately named 1960 suspense thriller, Psycho.

Next in line is the <u>patrol officer</u>, whose job it is to be professional and enforce the laws fairly without regard to a person's race, color, creed, religion, gender or gender orientation. If the law enforcement profession is broken, it was the patrol officer who broke it; which means the patrol officer has to fix it. Period.

Next in line is the <u>prosecuting attorney</u>, whose job it is to keep police officers in check by carefully reviewing each case before it reaches a judge or jury. It has always been my contention that the prosecuting attorney is most at fault when the justice system fails. Acquiescing to law enforcement is a gross dereliction of duty and engaging in the practice is reprehensible.

Next in line is the <u>juror</u>, whose job it is to always render an impartial verdict; or a verdict of "not guilty", in the event of malicious prosecution.

Next in line is the <u>judge</u>, whose job it is to ensure both the officer and prosecutor are as beholden to the Constitution as he is himself.

Last in line is a personal message to every police prospect, agency, patrol officer, prosecutor, juror and judge: Honor your oath, <u>period</u>.

CHAPTER THREE

9/11 and the Rise of the Oathbreakers

Listed below are ten reasons why placing one's full trust in the government to keep the homeland safe is so often a fool's errand:

1. Amache, Colorado
2. Gila River, Arizona
3. Heart Mountain, Wyoming
4. Jerome, Arkansas
5. Manzanar, California
6. Minidoka, Idaho
7. Poston, Arizona
8. Rohwer, Arkansas
9. Topaz, Utah
10. Tule Lake, California

WWII Japanese Internment Camp: Topaz, Utah

I was just three years old in 1963 when President John F. Kennedy was assassinated by Lee Harvey Oswald. A part of me still remembers watching men in dark suits and darker cars racing to and fro on the old black and white TV set in the living room of our home in Philadelphia. I still remember where I was standing in the living room when I watched the broadcast; the same way I still remember where I was standing on September 11, 2001 when the towers were hit, and later when they fell.

In response to the attacks, President George W. Bush created a bureaucratic behemoth called the Department of Homeland Security (DHS). Tom Ridge, former Pennsylvania Governor, was confirmed as the department's first Cabinet Secretary. DHS was an agency that some believed could have been modeled after another bureaucratic behemoth committed to rooting out enemies of the state: the former Soviet Union's Committee for State Security, or KGB. In truth, they were both omniscient monstrosities and, therefore, not all that dissimilar.

Soon thereafter, President Bush began the so-called "War on Terror" in earnest and ordered tens of thousands of service members into battle. Also in response to 9/11 was a decision made by a number of civilian law enforcement agencies to cast aside their traditional command and control structures in favor of one more closely aligned with that of the U.S. military.

Under the new civilian command and control structures, the once-ubiquitous patrol officer was re-designated as either a private or corporal. Patrol supervisors wore sergeant stripes on their sleeves. Next were the lieutenants and captains. Finally, majors and colonels.

Agencies went so far as to reboot their academy and in-service training programs in the image of the military. Increased emphasis was placed on more conventional topics such as threat assessments and firearm/defensive tactics training. Decreased emphasis was placed on Fourth Amendment updates and how to enhance community relations. Missing was a basic understanding of how the latter could negate the need for the former.

There was something else going on, something that was known to most agencies but not often disclosed to the public: it was getting harder to recruit quality candidates. Jobs in law enforcement were relatively plentiful and the need to hire bodies was ever-present. About the only way to put enough officers on the street was for agencies to lower their hiring and training standards.

Massive amounts of government resources were poured into civilian law enforcement after the attacks, a mobilization of persons and materials not seen since WWII. Slowly, but surely, civilian law enforcement transitioned from domestic keepers of the peace to an occupying force of some 900,000 men and women engaged in nation-building.

Among countless other agencies, both the DHS and FBI were tasked with hunting down domestic terrorists before they could carry out further attacks on the homeland. It was a results-driven process. Even more so, it was a revenge-driven process. Where to start looking?

That one simple question had millions of possible answers, minus the all-too-obvious who had been excluded from consideration by political correctness. Now was the time to mobilize the oathbreakers to rid the land of as many of the remaining terrorists as practical.

Like the legendary phoenix, the oathbreakers arose from the smoldering ashes left over after the attacks. They were domestic Benedict Arnolds, the American Revolutionary War General turned traitor to his country. Perhaps even treasonous like William Bruce Mumford who, in 1862, tore down a United States flag and met his maker at the downstream end of a rope.

Oathbreakers raised their hand and swore an oath to protect and defend the Constitution of the United States, with their fingers crossed behind their back. The oath meant nothing, other than it was required to graduate from the training academy. On the street, the oath was seen as an impediment to breaking heads and was quickly set aside.

Oathbreakers set themselves apart from their more benign contemporaries by their trademark Ray-Ban sunglasses; shaved heads; authoritarian attitudes; a plethora of tattoos; and military-style vests bristling with the latest battle-tested gizmos and gadgets. Agency heads were naive to think that they could outfit a civilian in the accouterments of war and still expect them to behave with civility.

> Agency heads were naive to think that they could outfit a civilian in the accouterments of war and still expect them to behave with civility.

"Cry 'havoc'!" became a clarion call for a new generation of oathbreakers. Many of whom, ironically enough, served on foreign battlefields as a part of the War on Terror (contrary to popular opinion, service members - especially those who have seen combat - are not always well-suited for civilian law enforcement). Were they conflating military rules of engagement with civilian rules of engagement? Possibly. What is known is that these officers were gloved-up and looking for an enemy to fight. They found one in the Constitution.

These were gung-ho officers who were convinced that anyone not wearing a police uniform was either a terrorist or cop-hater.

Countless law enforcement agencies were willing to accommodate these all-too-real domestic tyrants. To do so they adopted - or simply looked the other way - a more aggressive style of policing. Metaphorically speaking, oathbreakers had been let off the leash.

Find the terrorists they did. Cartoonist Walt Kelly, the creator of the comic strip "Pogo", captured the essence of the government's soon-to-be victory over domestic terrorism when he wrote, "We have met the **enemy**, and he is **us!**"

Oathbreakers worked off the assumption that every man, woman, and older child in the United States was a potential terrorist. Except for themselves, of course. They remained virtuous, even though they were breaking heads and ruining lives. It was a necessary evil done in the name of protecting the homeland from evil terrorists.

Among the community of oathbreakers, few were more of a threat to civil liberties than George W. Bush's godforsaken creation, DHS. This would include its many "umbrella corporations". By their words and deeds, these transgressors of liberty acted as though it was the good and decent people of America who were the terrorists. The government was necessarily emboldened by this, ultimately using the attacks as a pretext to impose a de facto form of martial law which, in some ways, is still in effect.

The American people were going to be made to suffer for a federal government whose willful incompetence allowed the 9/11 terrorists to slip through the cracks. How else to explain a government that knew, among other things, there were men of Middle Eastern descent taking flight lessons to learn how to fly an airplane - but not how to land an airplane?

Because of gross incompetence by the government, along with the diligent work of the oathbreakers, Osama bin Laden's murderous legacy would soon be secured.

CHAPTER FOUR

See Something, Say Something

Asserting one's constitutional rights is not an act of terrorism.

Among the strategies that were developed by the fed-eral government to combat domestic terrorism was the creation and marketing of the catch-phrase "see something, say something". It was a slogan that would quickly become a part of the American lexicon, as well as a part of the American psyche. It was a slogan that many Americans would come to rue.

Never one to let a serious crisis go to waste, the politicians in Washington D.C. saw the 9/11 attacks as an opportunity to accumulate further power and control over the American people. To this end came a self-described "War on Terror"; governance by presidential fiat; passage of the Patriot [sic] Act; sinister and secretive "Fusion Centers"; increased domestic spying; warrantless searches and seizures of persons and property; abuse of FISA courts; suppression of dissent; and, predictably, the accelerated militarization of domestic law enforcement.

Unbeknownst to most Americans, the tragedy of 9/11 was, in a roundabout way, the fault of the late Secretary of State Warren Christopher and Deputy Attorney General Jamie Gorelick; both of whom worked for the Clinton Administration. The two worked hand-in-hand to erect a communications "wall of separation" between America's national intelligence and federal law enforcement agencies. This stifling of critical resources was put in place soon after the bombing of the World Trade Center in 1993.

Terrorist boogie men were seemingly everywhere. Recall how a sprinkling of talcum powder on a sidewalk, or a discarded handbag on the subway, would shut down some of America's largest cities. Many Americans became schizophrenic zombies, unable to function without the government's assurance that it would keep them safe. Almost overnight, the resolute slogan "In God We Trust" became the totalitarian-like slogan "We Trust Big Government More".

Despite this massive growth in the size and scope of the government over the intervening years, the 9/11 terrorists and their stated goal to stoke fear in the heart of every American has hardly abated. Even in death, Osama bin Laden continues to raise legions of devoted followers.

Operating in the open, even living and working amongst us, bin Laden's foot-soldiers have assumed the ubiquitous title of "oathbreaker"; the useful idiots inside both law enforcement and the military who, working in tandem, would go on to make "see something, say something" four of the most appallingly successful, freedom-killing words in the United States of America.

Clay County, Missouri Sheriff's Department

"I took a call, you're a suspicious person, and I need your ID!" a Clay County Sheriff's Deputy told the bewildered photographer on the steps leading to the Clay County Courthouse in Liberty, Missouri. "You told me you were a terrorist. I have it right here on my body cam!"

Incredulous, the man said, "I never told you I was a terrorist, deputy. I told you I was a tourist."

Beaver County, Oklahoma Sheriff's Department

Sheriff's Deputy Chris McMinn, an older tinhorn with a Horseshoe Mustache and goat roper hat, arrested a man for filming a natural gas holding facility from a road ditch alongside a rural Beaver County highway. McMinn got it all wrong, proving himself to be just another good ol' boy with a badge and a laissez-faire approach to the Constitution. (For purposes of clarification, this is not about whether an officer should respond to a "see something, say something" call for service. It is their job to respond. What is NOT their job is to respond with the intent of undermining the Constitution. THIS IS THE WHOLE POINT OF THE BOOK.)

Counter-terrorism expert, McMinn

McMinn first fumbled around with demands for the man's ID, suggesting on three occasions that taking pictures of private property was a crime. Whoa, cowboy! If filming private property were a supposed crime, why was the man not immediately arrested? To make a lawful arrest, McMinn only had to establish probable cause (51%). When a lawman suggests something is a crime three times in two minutes, it goes without saying that probable cause to make an arrest has already been established. So what was the point of demanding the man first surrender his identification, something the man would have been legally required to do after being taken into custody?

Imagine if McMinn were to apply this same kind of oathbreaker logic after witnessing a murder first-hand? "Well, partner, I saw what 'ya done and I'm gonna slap on these bracelets. But first I need 'ya to pony up some ID!"

Deputy McMinn was performing the Oklahoma version of the old "Texas two-step", by swapping out the steadfast legal doctrine of "lawful detention or arrest first, ID second", for the steadfastly unconstitutional doctrine of "ID first, or be unlawfully detained or arrested".

When pressed by the man to articulate a crime, McMinn had an "Aha!" moment and blurted out "TERRORISM! It's all I got to go with if you're not willing to identify yourself!" McMinn went on to arrest the man for refusing to show identification, a charge later amended by the sold-out local prosecutor to the catch-all charge of obstructing an officer. (By the way, McMinn, "terrorism" is a CATEGORY of crime, not a SPECIFIC crime.)

What a scam. Deputy McMinn was supposedly investigating "terrorism" (his word); however, saying it was terrorism did not make it terrorism. McMinn could have said he was investigating the kidnapping of the Lindbergh baby and the outcome would have been the same. For all McMinn knew, the man could have been conducting a random and unannounced environmental assessment of the facility. Or maybe the man was conducting a Fourth Amendment audit to see if Beaver County law enforcement would honor their oath? Would either explanation have mattered to McMinn? Likely not.

In reality, the "crime" being investigated was whether an American citizen would surrender their papers to an oathbreaker like McMinn. Failing to surrender one's papers is of far greater importance than actual terrorism. Speaking of which, whatever happened to the "crime" of terrorism that McMinn said he was investigating? Apparently, it went the same way as the passenger pigeon. Imagine that.

McMinn first detained the man without reasonable suspicion of a crime and subsequently arrested the man without probable cause - manufactured probable cause does not count - and got away with it. Oathbreakers nearly always get away with it because of corrupt agencies and sold-out prosecutors. Once empowered, there would be nothing to stop an oathbreaker from using an unwarranted demand for identification as a conduit to engage in targeted harassment.

That is EXACTLY what McMinn did to the man, saying almost immediately upon making contact, "I think I've seen you before, haven't I? We've talked before. I gave you my name the last time we talked." In a voice dripping with sarcasm, McMinn "encouraged" the man to post this latest encounter on Facebook. My thoughts are that McMinn's actions were purposeful, that he demanded ID hoping the man would refuse to identify in order to make a retaliatory arrest.

In a nutshell, standing in a ditch holding a camera in Beaver County, Oklahoma is committing at least four crimes: filming private property; failing to identify; obstructing an officer; and violating an ambiguous federal terrorism statute. Also, in a nutshell, is that Beaver County, Oklahoma Sheriff's Deputy Chris McMinn is an oathbreaker disguised as a law enforcement officer, who only managed to protect and serve bin Laden's legacy rather than the people of Beaver County.

This is what the terrorists wanted: Americans turning on one another, aided and abetted by the men and women of law enforcement. Look how well it worked in Clay County, Missouri, and Beaver County, Oklahoma. Look how well the strategy has worked across the country; including in Madison, a suburb of Huntsville, Alabama. Look how well the strategy has worked indeed.

CHAPTER FIVE

Officer Parker and Mr. Patel

There are good people and bad people.
A police officer is expected to treat them accordingly.

As he strolled through his son's upscale suburban neigh-borhood in Madison, Alabama, 57-year-old Sureshbhai Patel of India was enthralled by America!

Patel was on his second sojourn to the New World, having just arrived in America a week earlier to help take care of his grandson. Now, as he continued his morning walk, his mind tried desperately to understand what he was seeing. Wealth beyond imagination! All the creature comforts that anyone could ever hope to have. Is everyone this rich in America, he wondered? Patel would pause and marvel at the beautiful homes and manicured front lawns, so different from what he had left behind in India!

As he walked, Patel was being watched. A man was peeking through the curtains and growing fearful. "See something, say something" came to mind. Had the government not encouraged its good citizens to report suspicious activity, even if the activity had no apparent connection to terrorism? Operators and armed personnel were standing by to take the call. Better safe than sorry, right?

Sureshbhai Patel would soon meet two members of the Madison Police Department's "Welcoming Committee", one of whom was Patrol Officer Eric Parker.

It was shortly after the officers' arrival that an astute Parker asked Patel if he were out "looking at houses and stuff". Patel was confused. He managed to communicate that he was from India and spoke almost no English. He recited his son's house number, even pointing in the direction of the home when asked to do so by Parker.

"Looking at houses and stuff" in a Huntsville, Alabama suburb left the 115-pound Indian National and doting grandfather partially paralyzed. He was the victim of Parker's vicious "leg sweep", delivered just 90 seconds after Parker and his officer-trainee made contact.

Fear is a contagion, one that makes people think and act irrationally. Irrational people are the first to surrender their constitutional rights to the government, provided the government returns the favor by keeping them safe. In this case, it was someone's irrational fear and misplaced trust in government that resulted in a confused grandfather being brutalized by a government agent named Eric Parker. When others fear, others suffer.

Except for Eric Parker, who claimed that he never used a so-called "leg sweep" on Patel. Officer Parker said Patel "pulled away" from him four times as Parker was trying to pat him down for weapons. Parker was simply "helping Patel to the ground" when he "accidentally slipped" and landed on top of Patel.

Parker was subsequently fired but later rehired by the Madison Police Department. The charge of assault was dropped under orders from the State Attorney General. United States District Judge Madeline Hughes Haikala threw out the charge of assault at the federal level after two mistrials. She ruled against allowing the third trial, saying there was little likelihood another jury would be able to reach a verdict. In her Findings of Fact, Judge Haikala wrote the incident was mostly Patel's fault for leaving his son's house and not carrying identification.

Parker's attorney, Robert Tuten, said of Patel, "You come to the U.S., we expect you to follow our laws, to speak our language. Mr. Patel bears as much responsibility in this as anyone." Tuten then said of his client, "(Parker) is devastated, kind of worn down, relieved, and hopeful that he can somehow pull the pieces of his life together and move on."

Sureshbhai Patel continues to recover from the debilitating effects of a broken neck. It is unclear if he will ever be able to stroll around his son's neighborhood again.

While Parker has been fortunate to elude justice, the same system has denied justice to Mr. Patel. Both circumstances were the result of a man in the neighborhood seeing nothing, but going ahead and saying something, anyway. Sureshbhai Patel had become just one more casualty in America's post-9/11 war against itself.

CHAPTER SIX

Abuse of Authority

Oathbreakers don't fight crime. Oathbreakers
fight the Constitution, instead.

I would like to think that most law enforcement officers
are not intrinsically evil, or in some way predisposed to violence;
although given the apparent number of bad officers, my knee-jerk
reaction to always give law enforcement the benefit of the doubt is as
dead as Julius Caesar. Still, there are good cops amongst the bad and
conflating the two is patently unfair to the good ones. Yes, there are
good cops. I know because I worked with them day after day, year
after year.

These are the officers who are willing to confront extreme
violence, where evil lurks and profound darkness prevails: domestic
violence, mass shootings, or a multi-fatality car accident with tiny
bodies strewn about. Where officers are made to listen to a drunk
driver drone on about the damage to his car.

Being immersed in the law enforcement profession for almost a quarter-century has provided me two things if nothing else: legitimate street credentials and the ability to know how police officers think, often before THEY know what they are about to think. What I am hearing with my own two ears and seeing with my own two eyes has left me deeply worried.

Working the streets of America is the first generation of police officers who more or less came of age following 9/11. It is all they have known, having been inculcated with the notion that terrorism was the biggest existential threat to America. Most are mere youngsters whose brains would fall out if they knew the reason why us Cold-War Era "Baby Boomers" had to perform "Duck and Cover" drills in grade school.

While there will always be oathbreakers of every age and gender stirred in amongst good officers, this post-9/11 generation of oathbreakers seems different. By their actions and attitudes, these officers seem almost antithetical towards freedom. In short, they are too keen to antagonize, too quick to use violence, and too averse to holding themselves accountable in the same way as they hold the citizens accountable.

Furthermore, they are humorless, acting as though they hate the people they serve. Take a moment and check out the videos on YouTube. They will reveal shocking behavior; moreover, it does not seem to matter which agency or jurisdiction the officer hails from.

Oathbreakers are like-minded and tend to do the same thing whenever they show up at a call: posture menacingly, bark orders, and go straight to handcuffs or a Taser. Oathbreakers are consistent if nothing else. They are also master manipulators who know how to shrewdly shift the burden of proof away from themselves, only to exchange it for the suspect having to prove their innocence. This is to be expected when police officers brush aside requisite objectivity in favor of making the arrest.

These are "Stepford Cops", named after the 1975 cult-classic film, The Stepford Wives. One by one, the wives' personalities change. No longer capable of independent thinking, they become fixated on serving their husbands. Robotic behavior and blind obedience, dedicated to a single cause - no longer human.

A word of warning to every "Stepford Cop": NO ONE IS A POLICE OFFICER FOREVER! One day you, too, shall return to civilian life. So tread lightly, young Padawons, lest you find yourselves reaping that which you have sown.

> ...the two most powerful and transformative words in a police officer's vocabulary are not "or else", but "I'm sorry."

It would be helpful at this point to remind younger police officers - as well as a few older police officers - that the two most powerful and transformative words in a police officer's vocabulary are not "or else", but "I'm sorry." A smile and a cheerful wave, instead of a stereotypical frown and being the cheerless knave, are helpful too.

From the public's perspective, it appears that police officers are focusing too much time and energy enforcing what most look upon as trivial infractions: jaywalking; loitering; blocking the sidewalk; missing bicycle reflectors; or everybody's party favor, the burned-out license plate light, which pretty much renders the whole idea behind reflective license plates a moot point.

Except for minor children and newborns, I would add seatbelt violations to the list. It is the quintessential example of the government attempting to protect us from ourselves. Think of it as smoking in public. It is well-documented how a non-smoker's health is adversely affected by breathing second-hand smoke. Not to mention the stench that clings to the clothing of non-smokers the same way that leeches cling to the legs of swimmers at Etna Pond.

It becomes unreasonable when the government tries to ban smoking in one's own home. Similarly speaking, a car is a person's home on wheels and the main reason the government should mind its own business when it comes to whether a grown-up should wear a seatbelt. Besides, the only person who can get hurt is the person not wearing a seatbelt.

Moreover, oathbreakers will stop travelers under the pretext of not wearing a seatbelt when the traveler is, in fact, wearing a seatbelt. They have now empowered themselves with the ability to stop whomever they want, whenever they want, culminating in a demand for papers under the threat of arrest. Lawmakers are complicit with this deception by enacting seatbelt laws, first as a "secondary" violation (cannot be the sole reason to make a traffic stop), then sneakily changing it to a primary violation later on.

There is no question that the enforcement of seatbelt and other petty offenses will snag a wanted fugitive on occasion. I snagged my fair share, although at the time of the arrests I was enforcing misdemeanors. Enforcing a less-serious petty offense was outside the scope of my lawful authority as a South Dakota Game Warden.

Still, the enforcement of less serious infractions should never be done solely to justify an officer's existence, alleviate boredom, or as an excuse to use unreasonable force. Here are some examples of police officers using the enforcement of petty offenses as an excuse to use unreasonable force, sometimes for no reason other than the officer's feelings were hurt. In each of these examples, might the outcome have been different had the officers incorporated a sense of humanity into their decision-making process?

New York City, New York Police Department (NYPD)
Throughout its 175-year existence, the NYPD has consistently been one of the most corrupt and violent law enforcement agencies in the United States, the Chicago Police Department excepted. The current force of 38,000 NYPD officers has done little to dispel the reputation. Apologists for the agency like to fall back on the complexities of working the streets of New York City as justification for an officer's "mistakes".

That "CYA" attitude, and the anonymity provided by working in such a massive metropolitan area, are what contribute to the culture of corruption and violence. As in all large metropolitan police forces, oathbreakers in New York City are confident they will never be held to account. An air of invincibility is understandable given the number of people whose lives have been ruined - or taken - by members of America's largest and most violent street gang.

Why I have chosen not to include examples of the horrific abuse of the citizens over minor infractions by NYPD officers is a matter of not knowing where to start. A compromise is in order, so I will start and end with just one name: Eric Garner, the 43-year-old married father of six, who received the death penalty in 2014 for avoiding New York's excessive tax on cigarettes.

Being an entrepreneur, Garner sold "loose" cigarettes to any interested passerby, having purchased the cigarettes from an adjoining state where costs were far lower than in New York. A sky-high $6 tax imposed on each pack of cigarettes was intended to raise revenue as well as dissuade smokers from smoking, known to be a leading cause of heart and lung disease. Tragically, Eric Garner himself did not die from smoking cigarettes. Rather, he died from *selling* cigarettes. This ongoing level of senseless and unjustifiable police brutality - across the whole of the country, it would seem - has me seriously rethinking if the Revolutionary War's "Shot Heard 'Round the World" was worth the trouble?

Five years after Garner's death by asphyxiation, Police Detective Daniel Pantaleo - the instigator who used a banned chokehold to subdue Garner - was fired. Patrick Lynch, President of the Patrolmen's Benevolent Association of New York City, said in response to Pantaleo's firing, "Our police officers are in distress -- not because they have a difficult job, not because they put themselves in danger, but because they feel abandoned."

Lynch's words of support for the fired detective were in keeping with the police union tradition of defending one of its members, no matter what. At the press conference denouncing Pantaleo's firing, Lynch spoke not one word of support for Garner's family. This, too, is in keeping with police union tradition.

Independence, Missouri Police Department

Former Police Officer Timothy N. Runnels is a sadistic and brutal man. Runnel's actions during a 2014 traffic stop left 17-year-old Bryce Masters comatose and fighting for his life in a hospital. It was an attack representative of how quickly things can turn violent when an oathbreaker chooses to escalate a contact.

To maintain a sense of decorum, I refuse to write a more detailed account of the attack and Runnels' total disregard for the life of young Masters. It can be viewed in its entirety on YouTube and any subsequent judgment left in the hands of the viewer.

Consider yourselves warned.

In the unlikely event that an oathbreaker from Independence, Missouri is reading this account, let me make something clear: this is not a game. Law enforcement is a deadly serious trade, certainly for the officer but equally so for the person with whom the officer is interacting.

So, oathbreakers, the next time a motorist asks why they were pulled over or why they are being placed under arrest, do the right thing and answer the question.

Glendale, Arizona Police Department

Johnny Wheatcroft was the front seat passenger of a car that was parked in a Motel 6 parking lot. His friend was behind the wheel, while Wheatcroft's wife and young children were seated in the back.

They had been pulled over by Glendale Police Officer Matt Schneider for an alleged turn signal violation, yet Schneider chose to contact Wheatcroft instead of the driver. This was the first of several red flags. Officer Mark Lindsey was present at the scene as well.

Officer Michael Fernandez would arrive just minutes later. Johnny Wheatcroft would not stand a chance against these officers. Nor would he stand a chance against the five Glendale police officers who were soon to arrive at the scene of the stop.

Officers Schneider and Fernandez each had a history of misconduct, with Fernandez racking up the greater number of infractions. Officer Lindsey had no similar history of misconduct and was therefore without excuse.

Officer Schneider could have lawfully ordered Wheatcroft to step out of the car. Instead, he ordered Wheatcroft to surrender his ID. Doing so was the second red flag. Wheatcroft declined. Schneider again demanded Wheatcroft's ID. Wheatcroft again declined. Wheatcroft had just blundered into the bear trap that Schneider had sneakily set for him.

"Why do I have to show you my ID?" Wheatcroft countered. "I didn't do anything wrong." Wheatcroft was no saint - none of us are - but he was right. Absent a crime, an innocent passenger does not have to surrender their personal information to law enforcement.

The number of commands to relinquish the information is irrelevant. √ **(Under Stufflebeam v. Harris [2008] and U.S. v. Landeros [2019], innocent passengers do not have to identify themselves to law enforcement.)**

"We'll take you down to the station and fingerprint you," said Schneider in an attempt to intimidate Wheatcroft into surrendering his personal information. Another red flag. Next, Schneider said, "Passenger has to ID. We're on a traffic stop, brother!" Schneider had no intention of backing down - the reddest of red flags.

Wheatcroft held firm and the irascible Schneider continued to escalate. Things were not going according to plan, so Schneider decided it was time to force Wheatcroft out of the car.

In their haste to pull Wheatcroft from the car, neither Schneider nor Lindsey thought to undo Wheatcroft's seatbelt. Because of the seatbelt, it was nearly impossible for Wheatcroft to comply with Schneider's orders. "Stop resisting!" "Stop resisting!" both officers screamed over and over. Wheatcroft was not resisting the officers. He was still held fast by the seatbelt.

Above the din could be heard the distinctive crackling of a Taser and the cold ratcheting sound of stainless steel handcuffs. Wheatcroft would be tased nine more times during the brutal assault. "Relax!" "Relax!" the officers screamed over and over to a man who was being simultaneously beaten and electrocuted. "Relax!"

Each command to "relax" was followed by another plea from Wheatcroft to stop. Wheatcroft was being tortured at the hands of Officers Schneider and Lindsey. Johnny Wheatcroft's ordeal had only just begun.

By this time Wheatcroft was on his back on the ground, only now his legs were caught in the seatbelt. A redheaded child had to scramble over the passenger seat to untangle the seatbelt from around his father's legs. Wheatcroft felt the crippling sting of a Taser as he was rolled onto his stomach. More Glendale police officers joined the fray.

From inside the car could be heard the horrified screams of Wheatcroft's wife and children. Wheatcroft's wife grabbed a bag of unopened soda cans and pitched it at one of the officers. Officer Lindsey was struck in the head and knocked temporarily unconscious.

A look of terror on the face of a child, courtesy of the police.

Wheatcroft was still lying face-down on the ground when Schneider pulled down Wheatcroft's shorts and underwear. In front of his family, Schneider first kicked, then tased, Wheatcroft in the testicles. Schneider mocked Wheatcroft by telling him that he deserved to be kicked in the testicles for not settling down. Schneider later said that he never tased Wheatcroft in the testicles. "I tased him in the groin," Schneider clarified.

When an officer went against policy and tried to yank the pair of barbed Taser hooks from Wheatcroft's back, Schneider scoffed and said, "Relax! Stop being a big baby!" This from an officer who the Glendale Police Department would roll out from time to time for special media appearances, including the television show Cops.

On and on the violence went, relenting just long enough for officers to throw Wheatcroft into a cage in the back of a police car.

Like his wife, Wheatcroft was charged with two counts of felony battery on a police officer. One has to appreciate the sick irony of the Wheatcroft's being the ones who were charged with felony battery. An independent investigation would later reveal that Schneider was never in a position to observe the car and the resulting turn signal violation. Schneider lied and freedom died, right there in a Motel 6 parking lot.

The Glendale Police Department later released a carefully-worded statement which placed most of the blame for the violence on the Wheatcrofts. The Wheatcroft children were unavailable for comment.

Officers Schneider, Lindsey, and Fernandez each received a letter of reprimand for their role in Wheatcroft's violent arrest; additionally, Schneider was suspended without pay for three days. At the time of writing, all three officers were still gainfully employed with the Glendale Police Department.

Texas Department of Public Safety

On the afternoon of July 10, 2015, Illinois native Sandra Bland was stopped near the small town of Prairie View, Texas for failing to use a turn signal while changing lanes. Three days later Bland was dead, having hanged herself in her jail cell. It was a case of police brutality

that would soon garner the attention of every major newspaper and media outlet in America.

What had started amicably quickly devolved into a verbal and physical roadside scuffle after Texas State Trooper Brian Encinia ordered Bland to extinguish her cigarette. She refused, saying to the trooper that she had every right to smoke in her own car. An enraged Encinia pulled his Taser and yelled, "I will light you up! Now get out of the car!"

Despite his repeated threats of violence, a remarkably calm Sandra Bland asked Encinia, "Why am I being apprehended? You're doing all this for failing to signal? You're gonna drag me out of my own car for failing to signal?" Encinia could have attempted to de-escalate the rapidly deteriorating situation (of Encinia's own making, remember) by simply saying "I'm sorry, ma'am. Would it be alright if we started over?" — but sadly chose not to.

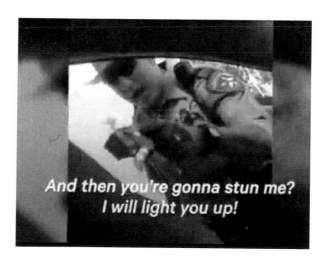

Pride along with an apparent lack of humanity contributed to the death of 28-year-old Sandra Bland, the young woman who was

looking forward to starting her new career in the state renowned for its resilient battle cry, "Remember the Alamo!"

Oregon State Police and Corvallis, Oregon Police Department

Oregon State University student Genesis Hansen is a petite, 21-year-old African-American college student, whose actions on October 13, 2019 drew the attention of Oregon Senior Trooper Kelly Katsikis. Corvallis Police Officer Donald Sheldon soon joined the pair, as did five more Corvallis police officers.

Ms. Hansen was already lying handcuffed on the ground by the time the full complement of backup officers arrived. Seven gloved-up police officers to help subdue a tiny, 95-pound college student who Trooper Katsikis had stopped for allegedly riding her bicycle on the wrong side of the street. Do any of these officers believe in their heart that what they did that day was good police work, or is that a rhetorical question?

Katsikis' and Sheldon's post-arrest conversation was captured on Katsikis' body camera. It seems the two Romeos had beaten up Ms. Hansen because they assumed her reluctance to show ID was her trying to hide the existence of an arrest warrant.

Katsikis

No, guys, Ms. Hansen had no outstanding arrest warrants. She was trying to reason with Katsikis after it became apparent he had misread the law.

As an aside: a commonality shared by so many police officers is an overwhelming urge to check everyone they contact for outstanding warrants. This is the reason oathbreakers are so desperate to get their hands on a person's ID - date of birth is paramount - to the point where they will unlawfully detain and/or make an unlawful arrest simply to find out. To describe the urge as pathological would be an understatement.

Not knowing how to proceed is fairly characteristic of an oathbreaker. The reason the contact with Ms. Hansen went sideways is that a clueless Senior Trooper Katsikis escalated the situation and was unable or unwilling to de-escalate the situation. All roads lead back to a lack of character and puffed-up pride, worn on the officer's sleeves like chevrons.

New Jersey State Police

Troopers Joseph Drew and Andrew Whitmore did the unthinkable to a young driver whom they had pulled over for a minor traffic violation. Having used the alleged odor of marijuana as probable cause to search the car, the troopers expanded the scope of the search to include the young man's cherries and dingleberries, right then and there along the side of the road. "If you think this is the worst thing I'm going to do you," Trooper Drew threatened, "you have another thing coming, my friend!"

Although no marijuana was found - either in the car or on his person during the highly-invasive search - the incident nonetheless served a purpose in two ways: making the case for legalization of marijuana and making the case to live somewhere other than the Police State of New Jersey.

Dallas County, Texas Sheriff's Department

Sheriff's Deputy Christopher Leon Smith stopped a van occupied by a male driver, along with the driver's wife and 2-year-old child. In a video of the encounter that was taken by the driver's wife, Deputy Smith can be heard ordering the driver to step out of the van after the man voluntarily announced that he possessed a Concealed Weapons License. √ **(Under Pennsylvania v. Mimms [1977], an officer can lawfully order the <u>driver</u> to step out of the car for purposes of officer safety. It does <u>not</u> give the officer carte blanche to do whatever he wants.)**

Even though the driver made no furtive movements and never brandished a weapon, both his honesty and request not to be separated from his family were rewarded by him being dragged violently from the van by several sheriff's deputies. A steep price to pay for having a burned-out license plate light.

Egg Harbor Township, New Jersey Police Department

On the afternoon of May 11, 2019, Patrol Officer Steve McKenney ordered a front-seat passenger to step out of the car. √ **(Under Maryland v. Wilson [1997], an officer can lawfully order the <u>passenger(s)</u> to step out of the car for purposes of officer safety. It does <u>not</u> give the officer carte blanche to do whatever he wants.)**

The passenger hesitated, telling Officer McKenney that he was scared of the police. He also said he suffered from epilepsy and was prone to seizures. When a second oathbreaker showed up, it was game over for the passenger.

McKenney placed the passenger under arrest - with no explanation of what he was being arrested for - and again ordered him to step out of the car. A livid Officer McKenney reached through the open passenger window and unlocked the door from the inside. The passenger was dragged from the car, pummeled by both officers, and smashed face-first into a side window of the car.

Nearly unconscious and foaming at the mouth, the prostrate man lapsed into a series of violent spasms as the two Egg Harbor Township police officers kept him pinned to the ground. Such untoward violence for committing the infraction of flicking cigarette ash out the window.

Stockton, California Police Department

On September 15, 2015, a young male patron waiting for a bus was assaulted by a police officer wielding a baton. Cries of "He's just a kid!" rippled through the disbelieving crowd.

Unable to take the "passively resisting" teen into custody, the officer made a frantic call for backup over his portable radio. Soon there were nine Stockton police officers on scene but not a hero among the bunch. Five of the officers swarmed the teen and took him forcibly to the ground. Once handcuffed, the officers dragged the young man to his feet and carted him off to a cage.

For each of these cowards, pettiness had become a priority; with the resulting violence driven by out of control egos and an overwhelming need to dominate another human being. It was animalistic behavior that started over an alleged jaywalking infraction.

Chester Township, Pennsylvania Police Department

"If they pass it, they will come" is a parody of the famous line, "If you build it, he will come", from Kevin Costner's 1989 movie, Field of Dreams. Costner's character builds a baseball field in his cornfield, in the hope of reuniting with his deceased father. It ends with the two tossing a baseball to and fro in one last game of catch.

There is no such happy ending for the residents of Chester Township. The City Council passed an ordinance, later ruled unconstitutional, prohibiting loitering in a "high drug activity area" and left its interpretation and enforcement in the hands of the Chester Township Police Department - without the benefit of an enforcement policy.

Soon the police came and brought with them a willingness to use violence against any person whom the officers arbitrarily deemed were loitering in one of these so-called "high drug activity areas". It was a willingness that included harassing residents who stood on the sidewalk in front of their own homes.

Residents of a predominantly black neighborhood took the brunt of the harassment, having been terrorized into submission by a gang of armed lunatics. Officers arrested several members of the same family for loitering in front of their home two days in a row. During one encounter, officers attacked a family member as he tried to walk into the home, first using a Taser, then pitching the man headlong over the railing of the front porch like a sack of potatoes. "What's the matter?" an officer said in response to a family member's tortured plea. Pointing first toward the home, then the sidewalk, the officer sneered, "He lives there, not here!"

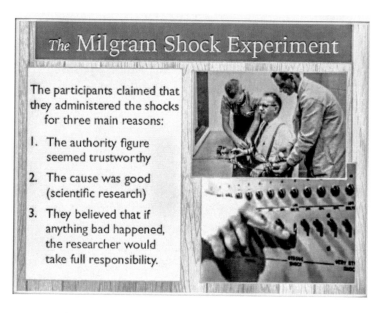

The Milgram Shock Experiment

The participants claimed that they administered the shocks for three main reasons:

1. The authority figure seemed trustworthy

2. The cause was good (scientific research)

3. They believed that if anything bad happened, the researcher would take full responsibility.

Does the word "Nazi" come to mind? It should.

In WWII Germany, "Befehle sind befehle!" was how obedient little Nazis justified their crimes against humanity. "Orders are orders!" is the same excuse used by today's oathbreakers to justify their own crimes against humanity, including the goose-stepping order-followers from Chester Township.

What is occurring in Chester Township is a confirmation of the results disclosed by the "Milgram Shock Experiment". In 1961, Psychologist Stanley Milgram at Yale University conducted experiments on the conflict between obedience and personal conscience. Milgram's experiments were an attempt to shed light on why the average Deutschlander was able to commit such atrocities during WWII.

Consistent with a German culture that promotes strict discipline, those affiliated with the Nazi Party claimed they were simply following orders. They were told what to do, so they did it - unquestioningly. It was a pattern of obedience to authority that led up to the authority reserved for Herr Hitler, Milgram concluded.

There was little chance the pattern of obedience to authority would have surpassed the authority reserved for Herr Hitler. Of the many titles the paperhanging mama's boy from Linz, Austria acquired during his 12-year reign of terror, none were more esteemed than "Supreme Law Lord".

For those interested, Milgram astutely recorded his test subjects as they begrudgingly obeyed nearly every one of the assistant's orders to inflict pain on another human being (their anguished cry of pain was staged). It is chilling to watch, nonetheless.

> **...superior numbers and too-easily-deployed Tasers make it far more likely that oathbreakers will resort to violence.**

Know this: like wolves, oathbreakers are predators and travel in packs. This is what gives them the confidence to act so aggressively and overstep their lawful authority. What happened to Johnny

Wheatcroft in Glendale, Arizona, and to the family members in Chester Township, Pennsylvania, is happening across America. Regardless of the circumstances, superior numbers and too-easily-deployed Tasers make it far more likely that oathbreakers will resort to violence.

CHAPTER SEVEN

It's Only a Camera

When the government focuses its cameras on us, we're told it's for our own good. When we focus our cameras on the government, we're told to put our hands behind our back.

Being harassed for standing still on a public sidewalk happens quite frequently to activists, most often when they film the police. No surprise there, since the police hate being held accountable. Cameras have exposed widespread corruption and dangerous incompetence in American law enforcement, without regard to agency or jurisdiction.

Despite cameras being everywhere in American society, including tens of millions of cell phone cameras tucked away in pockets and purses, people still freak out at the sight of a camera pointed in their direction.

I get that people can be put off by the thought of their image being captured by a stranger's camera. What I will never get is the way that so many people are put off by the thought of a stranger capturing the image of a building. This is still the United States, right?

"911, what is your emergency?" "There's a guy standing on the sidewalk filming our building, and he's making the employees feel uncomfortable! Please hurry!" How disheartening the number of Americans who have been led to believe that taking pictures of a privately-owned building without permission is a jailable offense. Oathbreakers and their government handlers are delighted.

With each panicked phone call to 911, these Americans are waving the flag of surrender and ceding their peace of mind to bin Laden. How dare they give in to the fear; and how dare they use that fear to try to weaken the resolve of the American people overall. Not a single American took part in the attacks, so why have we chosen to turn on one another rather than the terrorists?

Some go even further, insisting that taking pictures of government buildings is a jailable offense. Law enforcement certainly seems to think so, judging by their sometimes violent reaction to their workplace buildings being filmed or photographed. How comforting to know that buildings in the United States of America are worshipped with the same religious zealotry as those who worship the Golden Temple of India.

One camera vs. seven guns seems fair.

Putting buildings before people is reminiscent of the days when the former Soviet Union handed down death sentences to any who were caught taking pictures of the Kremlin. Assigning more value to bricks and mortar, rather than flesh and blood, is the kind of depraved thinking that serves only to cheapen the value of life, liberty, and the pursuit of happiness. Thanks to the government, America has become a safer place for waste water treatment facilities and their sewage lagoon counterparts. I take comfort in that as well.

It does not stop at buildings, either. Try taking a picture of a police car and see what happens. Government-owned Crown-Victorias have more intrinsic value than God-owned human beings. One does not have to be a believer to grasp the danger this poses to freedom. Oathbreakers are helping to make this dystopian future a reality every day.

For civil rights activists, this is far more than a fight for individual freedom. Theirs is a movement committed to fundamentally changing America's love affair with fear. What stands in their way are frightened sheep and their government shepherds, committed to the fight against terrorism by breaking open the heads of their fellow Americans. Oathbreakers and their government handlers are delighted.

CHAPTER EIGHT

Tiparillo John and the Growing Disconnect

"Sometimes there's justice. Sometimes there's just us."
- Slogan associated with the thin blue line flag -

Say hello to "Tiparillo John". Tiparillo John worked for the Lexington, Kentucky Police Department and later transferred to the Jefferson County, Kentucky Police Department, which subsequently merged with another agency to become the Louisville Metro Police Department. He retired in 2014, then hired as a full-time employee with the Jefferson County Sheriff's Office in an unknown capacity.

Not long ago, Tiparillo John posted a video on his YouTube channel, named "Real Police Talk". Tiparillo John shared his thoughts on activists and bragged about having falsely arrested one.

Tiparillo John enjoyed a $4 cigar as he smugly recounted a story where he violated the civil rights of a free human being. This one's for you, T. J., 'ya sarcastic smoke pole! These are your words. You spoke 'em, you own 'em:

"Putting one activist in jail at a time. Going on down the list. They're idiots. These current activists are basically a bunch of malcontents. Low education, usually. Have been arrested and have police records. Just angry and are therefore going to make mistakes. Just not smart, doing it for all the wrong reasons. Doing it because they have a vendetta. Never going to work, right? No one's gonna be on their side because, generally, they're not the greatest people in the world. They're really not. Place(d) him under arrest and he's not compliant, so I grabbed his arm to put it behind him to, uh, hand-cuff him. He stiffens up, I put him against the wall and put him in a wrist lock. And I gently tell him, I persuade him to go along with the arrest. If he doesn't comply, it's just really going to get worse. 'You're under arrest, and you're going to get arrested, however I need to do, whatever I need to do, to arrest you!' So I use minimal force to put him up against the wall and whisper sweet nothings in his ear. He, of course, immediately complies. Now, all this is recorded on his phone. Okay? It is evidence, okay? It is evidence of a crime, so I book his phone into evidence. And I take him to jail and I booked his phone into evidence. So, anyway, court case comes up a few weeks down the road. Meanwhile, he's got no phone. The first two times it comes up, I wasn't able to make it. We had to postpone that, alright? So he postpones. Meanwhile, he's without his phone. That's a real pain in the [expletive]! He's got these charges hanging over his head. We merge the resisting arrest, that's fine, he was charged with, and I always like to charge them with it. For, um, several reasons. The next time a police officer has to deal with 'em, they end up having to hate 'em or hurt 'em. Real Police Talk! I actually have a ton of these types of stories. Not some self-proclaimed moron, [expletive] off because he's been arrested a few times. That's not really someone who's going to audit the government, ya know! (Now speaking as the activist)...'I'm going to show the government doing wrong stuff because they correctly arrested me, and I'm [expletive] off!'"

"So that's the first one I schooled, that I destroyed, that I owned!"

Tiparillo John spoke over 400 words without once mentioning the crime the activist had allegedly committed prior to his arrest for resisting. It would have taken Tiparillo John only four words at the beginning of the screed to put his actions into some semblance of context: "I arrested him for...". The fact is there was no crime until you showed up, was there T. J.?

This is the new normal for American law enforcement: make an arrest for the sake of making an arrest, without probable cause, only because the officer cannot tolerate what the citizen is doing in relation to the officer's best interest. (What is the point, may I ask, of requiring months of training when the only thing that oathbreakers seem to remember from the academy is how to shoot, tase, demand ID and make unlawful arrests? One day of training, with plenty of time left over to hit the local nightclubs, should do it.)

It is because of such openly-brazen oathbreakers like Tiparillo John (and his ilk) that the law enforcement profession has come under a much higher level of scrutiny from the public, scrutiny that is most often accompanied by a gut-level sense of distrust and betrayal. One might think this kind of public blowback would incentivize police officers to be more respectful. In reality, it has only managed to make good police officers better. It has not changed the behavior of an oathbreaker like Tiparillo John, at least not appreciably. In some ways, their behavior has gotten worse.

This unscrupulous and sometimes bizarre behavior has led to a growing "disconnect" between law enforcement in general and the people they serve. An "us vs. them" mentality that has become too prevalent among too many police officers. This is in stark contrast to what the father of modern-day policing, Sir Robert Peel, wrote back in 1829 with his "Nine Principles of Effective Policing".

In his Second Principle, Sir Peel wrote: "The ability of the police to perform their duties is dependent upon public approval of their existence, actions and behaviour; and on their ability to secure and maintain public respect."

Officer Shaeffer of the Abilene, Texas Police Department is representative of the disconnect.

Sir Robert Peel was warning future generations of police officers to avoid engaging in conduct unbecoming of an officer, lest they put at risk the support of the community. In contemporary terms, Sir Peel was warning against the "disconnect".

Some observers have hypothesized that the existence of the disconnect is due to the complexities inherent in today's policing. While this may play a role, complexity alone is neither a reason nor an excuse for police misconduct. A task's relative complexity requires caution, not carelessness; especially in a profession like law enforcement, where the consequences of carelessness can be catastrophic.

More to the point, it is the officer's own set of personal values that will usually determine whether a disconnect manifests over time. For instance, does the officer view others with a sense of humanity or inhumanity? The former promotes humility, while the latter promotes hostility. With whom would the public prefer to interact? Would they prefer to interact with an idiot cop like "hate 'em or hurt 'em" Tiparillo John? A more important question is "With whom would parents prefer to interact with their children?"

This may explain why some police officers reject the notion that they are subservient to the public. If not the public, to whom are they subservient? Without a basic understanding of their role as public servants, these officers are very likely to become "agent provocateurs"; in other words, officers who choose to manufacture conflict rather than foster relationships. These are the officers who taint the law enforcement profession as a whole, who abuse their authority and mostly get away with it. Furthermore, they seem to enjoy it.

Take note of the videos that go "viral" on the Internet, the ones that show a police officer changing a tire or line-dancing with "Mr. Shlotsky's preschool class". Although the officers seen in the videos are the ones who seem to "get it" in terms of humility and service to their communities, it cannot change the fact that they are engaged in full-blown damage control. For the level of distrust that now consumes the law enforcement profession - courtesy of the oathbreakers - is such that an officer is heralded as a hero for simply doing his or her job and being professional.

Another personality trait that oathbreakers share in common is being emotionally invested in their role as peacekeepers, to the point where they become obsessed with their sense of self-importance. This is the point of no return, where an oathbreaker loses their ability to maintain either a sense of perspective or a sense of self-control. Over time they will act less like peacekeepers and more like Judge Dredd, the fictional dispenser of justice in a dystopian society. Although his methods were brutal, Judge was at least meting out justice on those who had it coming.

Granted, the law enforcement profession was never intended to be warm and fuzzy; neither was it intended to be cold and distant. It should meet somewhere in the middle, with officers placing emphasis on being polite and professional until circumstances dictate otherwise. Contrary to popular belief, the measure of an officer's success is not how many complaints they can generate during an 8-hour shift.

Officers whose behavior helps foster the disconnect - and their no-account administrators who allow it to fester - are actually making their communities LESS safe by alienating the very same people they rely upon to solve crimes. Who can possibly benefit from that, other than the criminals?

What the following accounts have in common is how easily they could have been avoided or resolved if only we would stop talking past one another. If only we would see each other as fellow human beings. It has to start somewhere.

Harris County, Texas Sheriff's Department

What in the world was Sheriff's Deputy Gunter thinking when he told an activist that he hoped the activist would get run over by a car? Or that he hoped the activist would break the law to give Gunter a reason to take him to jail? Or when he sarcastically told the activist that he couldn't care less about the law?

Deputy Sarcastic

I could never have gotten away with talking down to a citizen the way Gunter did. Nor would I have wanted to. By his actions that afternoon, Deputy Gunter had proved to the world the existence of the disconnect. By his actions that afternoon, Sheriff's Deputy Gunter had BECOME the disconnect.

Williams County, North Dakota Sheriff's Department

We should all lament the current state-of-affairs of American law enforcement after 9/11. Police investigating a report of "suspicious behavior" is all the rage; a term defined by 900,000 police officers, each with their own interpretation of what is or is not suspicious behavior. Not only do they get to pick and choose what is suspicious, but they also reserve the right to accept or reject the explanations they receive.

Take, for example, what occurred when a citizen tried to familiarize himself with the offices and services available inside the Williams County Courthouse in Williston. Also, as he sat quietly in the back of a courtroom observing a civil trial. Along came three determined oathbreakers - two of whom were decked out in regalia normally reserved for wartime - led by the crotchety pot-bellied Sheriff's Deputy, Royce Crone.

Crone and a gloved-up order-follower.

It was a disturbing display of abuse of authority, whereby three so-called "peace officers" forced an American citizen - under the threat of extreme violence - to leave the courthouse for engaging in behavior that the oathbreakers said was "not normal". Who needs to articulate a crime when the government can just say "not normal" to ruin someone's life?

What could be more demonstrative of the disconnect than a gloved-up order-follower ready for the battlefield to say, "We don't need a reason. We told you to leave, so you need to leave" to an American citizen exploring a county courthouse?

Thanks for nothing, Williams County, North Dakota Sheriff's Department tyrants. May all your winters be a living h*ll from now on.

Weld County, Colorado Sheriff's Department

Deputy Tanner has an ego bigger than the State of Colorado, with character flaws as deep as Arizona's Grand Canyon. If this is the best Weld County has to offer, then shame on you Sheriff Reams.

Overpaid parking lot attendant.

Tanner rolled up to the scene of a reported trespass as though he were the King of Weld County. He was rude, unprofessional, and a bully from the outset. Officers like Tanner make no effort to be reasonable because they know they don't have to be reasonable. Nor do officers like Tanner even want to be reasonable.

A man had walked onto a Weld County parking lot in broad daylight to photograph two wrecked sheriff's cruisers that were parked along the auction line. There was not a single sign posted anywhere in sight warning visitors that it was a criminal offense to enter the lot without permission. Besides, as a taxpayer, how could the man be accused of trespassing when the property carried the same guaranteed right of access as the Weld County Courthouse?

Tanner detained the activist for the alleged crime of trespassing and threatened to tase the activist if he did not submit to being handcuffed. He ordered the activist to sit on the ground like a dog when it turned out that the activist was simply too large to be handcuffed behind his back. Tanner even threatened to arrest the man on a felony charge of trying to gain entry into one of the cruisers.

After a brief consultation with a supervisor, Tanner told the activist that he was being charged with 3rd-degree trespass and instructed a second officer to write the ticket. It is my understanding that the Weld County prosecutor has elected to take the case to trial.

Where in any of this sound and fury was there a crime, either against a person or property? It should have been handled with a friendly handshake between gentlemen. Then again, we are talking about Deputy Tanner, the oathbreaker who was willing to use violence to protect the best interest of a parking lot.

Warren, Michigan Police Department
Warren Police Sergeant J. Wolfe and two patrol officers approached an activist (now standing on the sidewalk) after receiving a "radio run" about a man causing "alarm" for filming at City Hall. While there are far worse examples of bad policing in America, what struck me most about Sergeant Wolfe was his callous and unprofessional demeanor. In particular, how the subordinate officers parroted Wolfe's remarks; either to curry favor or simply because they shared the same unprofessional mindset.

Sergeant Wolfe's inane and repetitive remarks centered on getting hold of the activist's ID, at one point telling the activist, "I wanna make sure you don't have any warrants or anything." When the activist refused, Sergeant Wolfe told him to leave the area. This was quickly followed by one of Sergeant Wolfe's subordinate officers also telling the activist to leave the area.

Sgt. Wolfe failed to set a good example for his subordinate officers.

In countless similar interactions, oathbreakers like Wolfe would have threatened the man with arrest. This would include the usual list of manufactured crimes: refusing to ID; obstructing an investigation; loitering; blocking a sidewalk; and/or failing to obey a "lawful order".

This back and forth continued until a frustrated Wolfe said, "Then leave. Get outta here. You can get outta here!"; to which a vexed subordinate added, "If we get another complaint, then we'll detain you until we can figure out what's going on!"

Great police work there, subordinate order-follower! Violate the man's constitutional rights in retaliation for making yourself look stupid on the Internet.

Towards the end of the encounter, before the activist walked away, he reminded Wolfe and his subordinates the importance of being professional while interacting with the public. "Try better... You could have (come up) to me respectfully, sir." Will oathbreakers pay attention?

DHS-Federal Protective Service (DHS-FPS): Houston, Texas

In October 2010, DHS disseminated a memorandum to its Field Offices reminding workers that it was legal for citizens to film the exterior and interior (within regulatory guidelines) of federal facilities from a public space. A second and similar memorandum was sent to the field in 2018.

Someone did not read the memos.

Psychotic and out of control is the only way to describe the conduct of a DHS-FPS officer, who aggressively approached an activist seen filming the exterior of an unspecified federal building. At times, the officer was within two feet of the activist's face - using his physical presence to force the activist to move back.

"What can we do for you?" the officer cried repeatedly as he threatened the photographer. "Hands! Let me see your hands!" Without the activist's camera acting as a silent witness, the officer would have unquestionably gone hands-on. The worst-case scenario was the maniac would have shot the activist. I am convinced of it.

Officer "UNSUB" finally backed down. There were two other DHS-FPS officers at the scene, yet neither attempted to intervene on the activist's behalf - courtesy of the disconnect.

DHS Office of Inspector General: Dallas, Texas

Special Agent Amy Owen approached an activist who was seen filming the exterior of the building where the Office of Inspector General is located. Agent Owen might as well have been reading from a script, her questions and accusations were that predictable.

Reading is fundamental, Agent Owen.

"Security had some concerns about you filming the building because it's a government facility," she told the activist. "Do you have authorization, because the employees are feeling uncomfortable knowing you're out here taking pictures?" "I do, actually!" the activist answered. With that, he handed Owen a copy of the First Amendment.

Agent Owen was trying to use feelings to trump the Constitution. It all flows from the 9/11 terror attacks and government workers like Owen thinking they deserve special perks and privileges. If this kind of weak-knees catering to personal feelings continues, there will come a day when no one will want to leave their home for fear of getting on someone's nerves.

There was one comment that Owen made that really piqued my interest. It was when she asked the activist if he had authorization to film the building. She was essentially asking if he had authorization from someone in the government before taking pictures.

This kind of thinking is incomprehensible on so many levels, for it would empower the government to approve what is already a constitutionally protected activity. It would further empower the government by requiring citizens to justify not just the ACT OF, but also the MOTIVE FOR, engaging in a constitutionally protected activity. This quashing of freedom would quickly spread to other levels of government, with the assurance that the government would do everything in its power to shut down every conceivable form of public accountability. This is going in the wrong direction, Agent Owen.

> ...permission REQUESTED of the government is permission DENIED by the government.

At the very heart of Owen's misstatement is that permission REQUESTED of the government is permission DENIED by the government. There would be no public photography of government facilities if Special Agent Owen had her way. On the other hand, business would be booming for the federal prison system.

Even more revealing was DHS Special Agent Amy Owen's stupefied reaction when the activist handed her the second set of papers. It was a copy of the 2018 DHS memorandum confirming a citizen's right to film the exterior of federal facilities, which the activist printed from the DHS website.

Apparently, DHS Special Agent Amy Owen had not read the memos.

Greenville, Texas Police Department

"Let me explain something to you, okay?" Lieutenant Starnes started in with an activist inside the public lobby of the Greenville police station. "You know, there's the possibility of people coming into a public building and taking pictures, to possibly case the place?" (that would have to be one stupid criminal, Lieutenant). Next was Starnes' all-too-predictable request for identification, which was a request that the activist politely declined.

Although the activist was not arrested - a rare exception - Lieutenant Starnes nonetheless followed the activist on foot after he left the building. All the activist had done to warrant such police harassment was peacefully engage in a constitutionally protected activity, on the inside of a public building bought and paid for by himself and every other taxpayer.

So, let me explain something to YOU, Lieutenant Starnes, okay? You work from facts, not "possibilities". Save the lectures for the criminals and stop treating a public building as though it were a private residence. Is that too much to ask from a public servant?

Los Angeles County, California Superior Court

A District Superior Court Judge issued a sweeping decree that prohibited taking photographs of "his" courthouse, including the outside! Furthermore, the decree prohibited taking photographs of the courthouse from any adjacent sidewalk or any sidewalk across the street from the courthouse.

In essence, the decree prohibited taking photographs of the courthouse regardless of where the picture was taken. He further ordered his lapdog sheriff's deputies to arrest any person they caught taking pictures of the courthouse and present them forthwith to his royal magistrate for gibbeting.

There is an adage that says nothing is more God-like than a general on the battlefield. The same can be said about a judge and his courtroom or, in this case, far beyond his courtroom.

U.S. Marshals Service: Houston, Texas

In a particularly troubling incident, an activist filming a downtown federal building was assaulted by several court security officers under the employ of Walden Security, a company under contract with the U.S. Marshals Service.

Virtually every security officer involved in the scuffle was a retired police officer. Their behavior that day was a testament to the government's self-inflicted descent into madness following 9/11. American citizens continue to be abused by their fellow citizens, working on behalf of a central government that knows no bounds when it comes to securing bin Laden's legacy.

In the meantime, the people sleep, unaware that a sinister boogie man is hiding beneath the bed. Patient to a fault, growing stronger each passing day. Still, the people sleep.

DHS-FPS and FBI Police: Washington, D.C.

It happened twice on the same day at the same place, by the same two federal law enforcement agencies. Two activists were harassed by FBI and DHS-FPS Police as they photographed the historic J. Edgar Hoover Building in Washington, D.C.

A very large FBI Police Officer, who refused to identify himself, was one of the first to make contact with the pair. Aggressive posturing and conduct unbecoming have become the norm for oathbreakers, especially after 9/11. Should we expect anything different from a government that treats its citizens like terrorists?

It was a tale told time and again. "Nervous" and "uncomfortable" government workers were acting on behalf of other "nervous" and "uncomfortable" government workers, in an attempt to deprive two American citizens of their constitutional rights. Given the government's habit of putting itself first and the citizens second, should the activists have expected anything different?

Police Department, Somewhere in the Police State of New Jersey

Now comes the story of a pompous New Jersey Police Sergeant, who told an activist that he would be arrested if his filming were to "disrupt the function of government". A frightful declaration with untold consequences for liberty. It further demonstrates just how far the government will go to protect itself from WE THE PEOPLE.

Santium Correctional Institution, Oregon Department of Corrections: Salem, Oregon

Oathbreakers think one-dimensionally. When in doubt, ARREST! At least give it the old college try and make up a crime if need be, just as long as someone is ARRESTED! This pre-programmed mindset to ARREST! took two corrections officers from Santium Prison to an unheard-of level of desperation.

Two activists were observed filming the facility from a public road right-of-way at the same time as fifty or so inmates walked around the perimeter of an outdoor track. Corrections officers first accused the men of planning a prison break. When that brilliant idea failed, one of the officers said, "You can't be filming the inmates without their written permission!"; which, in plain English, meant it was illegal to take a photograph of even one of the prisoners without their permission, let alone all fifty. I am speechless even now.

A constitutionally protected activity had elicited a knee-jerk, "You can't do that!" reaction from the government, for no apparent reason other than the government did not like what the men were doing (more on this later). This essentially granted the PRISONERS an expectation of privacy *OVER AND ABOVE* the expectation of privacy normally reserved for NON-PRISONERS. This is simply surreal. How dare the feckless government try to treat two free human beings as though they were a part of the prison's general population.

Fortunately, neither activist was ARRESTED!, although not for the lack of giving it the old college try.

Federal Drug Enforcement Agency (DEA): Las Vegas, Nevada
On March 22, 2017, a small group of activists was observed filming a DEA Field Office from a public sidewalk. They were soon approached by two DEA agents, both of whom launched straight into overt verbal and physical intimidation in an attempt to force the activists to stop filming.

These were two utterly corrupt government agents, disgusting pieces of totalitarian trash who showed how easily "men of power" can slip into the role of Ernst Roehm's Sturmabteilung, or SA Stormtroopers. It is because of agents like these two morons that comparing oathbreakers to Nazis is no longer just a cliche.

Fortunately, the activists maintained their composure during the short-lived encounter, considering the likelihood of violence by Herr Göring and Herr Himmler. Had they not, it is almost certain the DEA would have conspired with the Department of Injustice to sentence the men to spend the next few years under the day to day supervision of the Federal Bureau of Prisons.

If, as the saying goes, you cannot fight City Hall, try fighting the federal government with its unlimited resources. It would have been easier for the activists to pass Tiffany diamonds through their alimentary canals than to prevail against the government. The scariest part is that corrupt federal agents like the two morons know it.

DEA: Denver, Colorado

Did you know that it was against the law to film "private" cars in the United States of America? Any person caught filming "private" cars can expect a visit from local law enforcement. Never film private cars, because private cars have a reasonable expectation of privacy and the act of filming private cars violates their privacy. Only members of law enforcement are authorized to violate the privacy of private cars.

Did you know that it was against the law to film "private" license plate numbers in the United States of America? Any person caught filming "private" license plate numbers can expect a visit from local law enforcement. Never film license plate numbers, because license plate numbers have a reasonable expectation of privacy and the act of filming license plate numbers violates their privacy. Only members of law enforcement are authorized to violate the privacy of private license plate numbers.

On a more encouraging note, the government is considering carving out an exception for memorizing license plate numbers; however, jotting down license plate numbers on a piece of paper or the palm of a hand will remain strictly prohibited under penalty of law!

Edwards Air Force Base: Kern County, California

Two activists were unceremoniously arrested by security forces personnel after they were seen taking pictures of the "static display", an outdoor assemblage of Vietnam-era fighter jets located just outside the West Security Entrance.

Chances are this "miscommunication" between the activists and Air Force could have been avoided with the placement of just one conspicuous sign, which notified visitors in advance that it was a supposed violation of federal law to film publicly-displayed Vietnam-era fighter jets.

A source speaking on the condition of anonymity defended the oversight by Air Force officials, telling the Associated Press that recent cuts to the defense budget made it cost-prohibitive to buy one sign, four nuts, four bolts, four washers, one post-pounder, and two signposts. "It would have been a real budget-buster", the source said.

An on-scene security forces supervisor told the handcuffed men that they were only authorized to LOOK at the display; that any filming or photographing of the security entrance or distant flight line was expressly prohibited. Proving once again that a little knowledge is a dangerous thing, the security forces supervisor/amateur rocket scientist reversed course. He told the men that it was okay to film the display, as long as they did not film either the security entrance or flight line.

Say what? That was like telling the men that it was okay to film a boat on the water, as long as they did not film the water!

All charges were later dropped by federal prosecutors, but not before the men were threatened with the possibility of paying a substantial fine and spending upwards of eighteen months in prison.

Threatened with imprisonment inside a federal correctional institution for filming old fighter jets in public, after being arrested by the same government agents who intended for the public to photograph the display in the first place. How surreal.

So, the display was basically a set of decoys, meant to lure the photographers in like a couple of unsuspecting ducks? This is where my deepest regard for the United States military gets put on hold temporarily.

Not to be outdone, the men were contacted by agents from the FBI several months after their arrests. Both agents assured the men that the federal government did not consider either man to be a terrorist. As it turned out, that part of the field interview where the agents said they were members of the FBI's Joint Terrorism Task Force was no big deal after all!

To avoid future misunderstandings, the United States Air Force should consider changing the greeting on the beautifully-scrolled wooden sign that greets folks on their way to the Visitor Control Center. Swapping out the current greeting of "Welcome To Edwards Air Force Base!" with the new greeting of "Welcome To Edwards Air Force Base - Where We Arbitrarily Arrest Our Visitors!" seems appropriate.

Air Force Joint Base Elmendorf-Richardson: Anchorage, Alaska
It took barely one minute for an activist standing outside the base to be approached by two plainclothes members of the Military Investigation Unit. They, in turn, were followed by a military police officer and a uniformed FPS Officer from Bush's homegrown disaster, DHS.

One of the military investigators held his hands in the "interview, code yellow" position the entire time. This meant he was prepared to shoot and kill the activist. More frightening is the investigator's deadpan countenance which, when looked upon through my firearm instructor's eyes, meant he WANTED to shoot and kill the activist.

Just because it was the fourteenth anniversary of 9/11 did not grant security forces the authority to treat the activist as though he were the twentieth hijacker. Nor did it justify the FPS Officer threatening to "hook him up" and take him before a federal judge. "You're looking at a $100,000 fine and up to five years in prison!" the FPS Officer sneered. Let that sink in for a moment.

Randolph Air Force Base: Universal City, Texas

An activist standing well outside base property was detained by three heavily-armed security forces personnel, who had brought along a sleek military "bite" dog - just in case.

Several minutes passed before the activist was told his presence constituted a hostile act against the installation. A hostile act, as if he were standing outside Bagram Air Base in Afghanistan rather than outside a base deep in the heart of the Lone Star State.

Not surprisingly, the activist asked the airman if, by "hostile", he meant the United States armed forces were at war with America. It became the ultimate nightmare scenario when the airman had to think before he said no, the U.S. military was not at war with America.

Since then, a collection of activists have revisited Randolph Air Force Base to check whether or not base personnel amended their ways. They have not.

Army National Guard and Bowling Green, Kentucky Police Department

Independent thinking has never been a trademark trait for an oathbreaker. It was therefore not unexpected when the Bowling Green Police Department, acting on behalf of the Kentucky Army National Guard, told a photographer that he was banned from entering National Guard property for two years; even though neither he nor his young daughter had stepped foot onto the property.

During this particular encounter, a National Guard soldier told the father that he was not allowed to videotape the facility, declaring, "Yes, I defend your rights but, no, you're not allowed to videotape this facility!"

Just one more "You can't do that!" proclamation from someone who should have known better.

What had the pair done to elicit such a response? They were taking pictures of the M1 Main Battle Tank parked in front of the complex. While standing on a public sidewalk. In broad daylight. In the United States of America.

Fort Hood Military Post: Fort Hood, Texas

At least ten military police, two sheriff's deputies, and an unending stream of verbal intimidation are what greeted an activist filming the installation from a public easement.

Military police left the grounds of the installation (where they had authority) to harass the activist off grounds (where they lacked authority). In the meantime, the sheriff's deputies tried their best to apply federal military law to non-military state property.

Neither military nor civilian law enforcement knew what to do. When oathbreakers are in doubt about what to do, they usually just make an ARREST! So each entity defaulted into ARREST! mode, which is why the sheriff's deputies were on the phone with a supervisor. They were checking if they had the authority to ARREST! the activist for failing to ID. When in doubt about making an ARREST!, just DEMAND ID!

Back and forth they went, each deferring to the other's jurisdiction, hoping one would take that proverbial leap of faith and make the ARREST! Until, finally, both sides angrily relented and released the activist from custody.

Had he not been an experienced activist, one who knew how to stand his ground, the outcome would have been drastically different in my opinion. Still, the activist had come dangerously close to being thrown into a cage by officers who, regardless of the law or legal jurisdiction, so desperately wanted to make an ARREST!

Naval Air Station: Corpus Christi, Texas

Petty Officer Short: "You're not allowed to do that, sir! Under U.S. Code, you're not allowed to take pictures of a federal installation!" Petty Officer Trevino: "This is a military installation! You're not allowed to be filming anything or anything that happens on the base! So, you want me to call the CCPD? Do it legally?"

The call to the Corpus Christi Police Department was placed - and the two officers who responded to the call honored their oath! As for the TEN on-scene, and off base, U.S. Navy security personnel present, shame on you all.

Two citizens filming from a public sidewalk were confronted by members of the two most powerful government institutions in the United States: the U.S. military and civilian law enforcement. It was just another example of America's post-9/11 culture of fear, one that helped shape America's new national motto: non potes facere illud!

Joint Base Pearl Harbor-Hickam: Honolulu, Hawaii

Of the many civilian-military interaction videos that were reviewed, this is the one that I found most frustrating. An activist was a terrorist in the eyes of the U.S. Navy. That was pretty much the gist of it. Now, remember, base security personnel performing their due diligence is not the issue, otherwise they would be derelict in their duty. Rather, it is a matter of whether they honor their oath to the Constitution.

Putting base security aside, what they do NOT get to do is treat an American citizen the way they did. What they do NOT get to do is [expletive]can the Constitution. Perhaps the worst part about this and other civilian-military interactions is the angry and contemptuous attitude of base security personnel. They rarely see freedom in the eyes of activists, only the eyes of someone they would just as soon hurt or kill.

> ...(base security personnel) rarely see freedom in the eyes of activists, only the eyes of someone they would just as soon hurt or kill.

Regardless if the responding base security personnel are members of the military or civilian law enforcement, there is something about the way they hook their thumbs inside a load-bearing vest that I find particularly off-putting. So is spitting on the ground. Most off-putting is seeing the thin blue line flag sewn onto a military member's uniform.

Before this gets completely out of hand, may I suggest to the United States military that it deal with the plank in its own eye first, before it worries about the speck in the eye of a civilian? It is not off-base civilians who pose the greatest threat to base security, but the threat posed by on-base civilians and fellow military personnel.

When viewed in their entirety, how are these interactions between military personnel and civilians not examples of the War on Terror being brought back to the shores of America? It seems the mantra of "fight them over there, so we don't have to fight them over here" is nothing more than the Department of Defense and the ever-delightful DHS spoon-feeding garbage to the American people.

Oathbreakers, civilian and military alike, are ascribing nefarious motives to a lawful activity, one clearly protected by the Constitution. They are engaging in preemptive law enforcement and have surreptitiously enacted the concept of "PreCrime" ripped straight from the movie Minority Report. Check that. It is more like "Pre **NO** Crime" they are engaging in.

Convincing oneself that everyone else is a terrorist is the kind of foolish and monolithic thinking that turns citizens into sheep and part-time oathbreakers into full-time oathbreakers. Fear of terrorism is indeed disproportionate to reality* and is fast reaching the point of no return in the United States. By tomorrow, it will be even worse.

*According to Global Research, a person is 55x more likely to be killed by a police officer than a terrorist.

CHAPTER NINE

What's a Displacement Activity?

An innocent person has two options when they see a police officer exhibiting the first signs of a displacement activity: 1) run, and 2) run faster.

A **"displacement activity" is the spontaneous release of** nervous energy in a sentient creature, usually brought on by sudden anxiety. Numerous examples of a "displacement activity" can be found throughout the book.

To understand a displacement activity and how it relates to law enforcement, look no further than the typical interaction between an officer and an activist; in particular, an interaction where the officer demands ID - absent reasonable suspicion of a crime - and the activist refuses to comply.

An easily recognized example of a displacement activity is when a dog gets anxious and chases its tail. When a police officer gets anxious, he instinctively reaches for the mic clipped to his uniform shirt and requests backup.

"I don't know what I'm doing. Send backup!"

A displacement activity is deadly serious business for three reasons: they are fueled mostly by feelings of intense frustration or embarrassment; the officer knows he screwed up but intends to go forward with the unlawful detention anyway; and it portends violence once the "gang" has arrived. Remember "instigator Timmy" kicking the kid in the head?

Officers will take it a step further by adding "The suspect is being uncooperative and refuses to identify!" to the request. It conveys a sense of urgency and gives responding backup officers the impression that a fellow officer is in some kind of trouble. Why else would they have been summoned as backup?

It is a purposeful escalation to a situation that began as an unlawful detention, made by an officer who had no idea what they were doing.

CHAPTER TEN

Detective McFadden and the "Terry Stop and Frisk"

On October 31, 1963, in Cleveland, Ohio, a plainclothes detective named McFadden observed three men behaving in a suspicious manner. Detective McFadden approached the men and identified himself as a police officer. In response to McFadden's inquiry into their seemingly odd behavior, the men mumbled and avoided eye contact with the detective.

Based on his observations and longstanding experience, McFadden was able to articulate "reasonable suspicion" that led him to believe the men were casing a store prior to a robbery; which, if true, meant one or more of the men were armed.

Because of McFadden's keen eye, along with the discovery of an illegally concealed handgun, a career criminal would lend his last name to the landmark 1968 Supreme Court case, Terry v. Ohio - known informally as a "Terry Stop".

Terry was eventually convicted on the charge of possessing a concealed handgun. His attorney appealed the conviction, asserting that McFadden had violated his client's Fourth Amendment right against unreasonable searches and seizures; in particular, that McFadden lacked probable cause to search Terry. The Supreme Court disagreed - Terry's conviction would stand.

Its ruling predicated on McFadden's arrest of Terry, the Court held that in order to perform a lawful "Terry Stop", the officer must be able to articulate reasonable suspicion that a person has committed, is committing, or is about to commit a crime. Furthermore, the officer must have reasonable suspicion to believe the person may be armed and dangerous in order to perform a cursory pat-down for weapons.

Take note of how the Court included the phrase "about to commit a crime" in its decision. This was obviously included in the Court's Findings of Fact as a result of McFadden being able to articulate why he believed an armed robbery was about to occur. What the Court failed to take into account is the inherent ambiguity of the phrase "about to commit a crime". It afforded police officers the opportunity to substitute speculation for articulation; their imagination, in other words. This is what happened in the case study that follows.

Most are unaware that prior to Terry v. Ohio, nonconsensual police encounters required probable cause. Terry came along and lowered the bar to reasonable suspicion. Police have been abusing it ever since.

CHAPTER ELEVEN

Terry Stop and Frisk: How a Judge Got it Wrong

OXFORD ENGLISH DICTIONARY DEFINITION OF "SUSPICIOUS". ADJECTIVE. A feeling that someone has done something wrong, illegal, or dishonest <u>without having any proof.</u>

Before proceeding, I would ask that the names of these four men be remembered: Detective Brad Youngblut; Lieutenant Joseph Leo; Sergeant Christopher Curtis (all of the Des Moines, Iowa Police Department); and U.S. District Court Judge Charles Wolle, presiding over the Southern District of Iowa.

As discussed, under a Terry Stop and Frisk the officer must be able to articulate reasonable suspicion that 1) a particular crime has been committed, is being committed, or is about to be committed; and 2) the person may be armed and dangerous in order to perform a pat-down for weapons.

Try to determine if, at any point, the officers were able to meet either - let alone both - of the two legal burdens as required under Terry.

Named specifically in a federal lawsuit that fell under the purview of Judge Wolle, the three officers were accused of violating the First and Fourth Amendment rights of photographer Daniel Robbins, also from Des Moines.

Robbins was filming a police station from a public sidewalk when he was confronted by the officers. After having deemed Robbins' behavior "suspicious", Robbins was subsequently detained, his person searched, and his cameras seized without Robbins' consent, probable cause of a crime, or a valid search warrant.

Det. Youngblut

In July 2019, Judge Wolle dismissed the lawsuit, ruling that Robbins' behavior "created reasonable suspicion among the officers that he was engaged in criminal activity." Wolle further said that Robbins had been given "ample opportunity to allay the officers' suspicion." In October 2019, the ACLU of Iowa announced its intent to file an appeal on Robbins' behalf.

Judge Wolle's most egregious error was allowing a constitutionally protected activity, such as public photography, to rise to the level of reasonable suspicion of a crime. Not once during Robbins' detention did any of the officers articulate reasonable suspicion of a particular crime, managing only to toss out a few ridiculous and unsubstantiated conspiracy theories.

Moreover, even with reasonable suspicion of a crime, the officers had no authority to perform so much as a cursory pat-down for weapons without first articulating why they believed Robbins was armed and dangerous. Judge Wolle let the officers get away with conducting a full-blown SEARCH and SEIZURE which, lacking consent or a valid search warrant, could only have been performed under a probable cause arrest.

Countless questions remain unanswered. What, specifically, was the criminal activity that led to Robbins' detention in the first place? When Robbins asked Detective Youngblut to state the crime, the verbally-aggressive Youngblut changed the subject. Several times, as a matter of fact. Nor did Judge Wolle specify a crime in his Findings of Fact.

As noted, he used the term "engaged in" - as in the act of committing a crime - to describe Robbins' behavior at the time he was confronted; which, if even remotely true, failed to explain why Robbins was allowed to simply walk off afterward.

If the officers' actions were so legitimate as Wolle made clear in his decision, why was Robbins detained for ten long minutes before he was searched and his cameras seized as evidence? This is absolute proof the officers were on a fishing expedition. In fact, Sergeant Curtis told Robbins he was NOT being detained and that he should just "get lost".

Lastly, if the officers were on such solid legal ground, why did an officer threaten to arrest Robbins for loitering - other than to learn his identity? At the time of the threat, Robbins was surrounded by at least six officers and told repeatedly that he was not free to leave.

These are substantive facts that Judge Wolle either overlooked or refused to consider. Could it be that his ruling was based entirely on the fact that Robbins was observed filming a police station, something the Judge may have felt was improper? If so, did bias play a role in his decision, a fact that Judge Wolle failed to disclose?

Judge Wolle ultimately lent more credibility to speculation than he did to articulation. His misguided ruling allowed the officers to deprive Robbins of his constitutional rights, not because of what Robbins was *doing*, but because of what the officers believed Robbins was *thinking*.

Moreover, Judge Wolle ruled that Robbins was obligated to answer the officers' protracted line of questioning as a way to quell their uneasiness. Robbins had to prove his innocence, in other words, whereas the officers carried no legal burden at all. A presumption of innocence evaporated, right along with the rest of Robbins' constitutional rights.

If law enforcement officers are incapable of correctly applying the essential elements of a Terry Stop and Frisk, imagine what oathbreakers like Youngblut, Leo, and Curtis will do with the gift they have been handed by Judge Wolle? Not only will officers now be able to shut down public photography of police stations anywhere in the Southern District of Iowa, they will almost certainly try to extend Wolle's ruling to include ANY filming of police officers. This will effectively put an end to the public's ability to hold police officers accountable, a dangerous precedent in this day and age of escalating police violence.

Judge Wolle afforded three police officers a nonexistent right to privacy, while he similarly obliterated the First, Fourth, and Fifth Amendment rights of Daniel Robbins. Judge Wolle did more harm to Robbins and to the integrity of the Constitution than the three officers combined. How dare you, Judge Wolle, or should I say "the erstwhile Judge Roland Freisler" instead?

CHAPTER TWELVE

Tiny Tim and Suspicious Activity

What is suspicious to one person is everyday life to
someone else, which is why an element of a crime
is required <u>before</u> the police get involved.

How does an officer investigate something as malleable
and undefined as "suspicious activity", anyway? Technically speaking, police investigate CRIMES, not "suspicious activities"; the latter limited in large part to a consensual contact.

Think of it this way: when a citizen calls 911 to report suspicious activity - without specifying a crime - what they are essentially reporting to dispatch is something along the lines of "I don't know what they're doing, but I know I don't like it!"

Unsurprisingly, oathbreakers do the very same thing when they, too, see something they dislike, such as someone filming a Des Moines, Iowa police station. This is the crux of the matter, maybe the most important point to be made in the book; primarily, how oathbreakers of every stripe have gotten away with changing "reasonable suspicion of a particular crime" to "reasonable suspicion of something that I (or somebody else) do not particularly like".

...oathbreakers of every stripe have gotten away with changing "reasonable suspicion of a particular crime" to "reasonable suspicion of something that I (or somebody else) do not particularly like".

This may sound far-fetched, but rest assured it is nothing of the sort. This has become yet another "new normal" for American law enforcement after 9/11, one that corrupt agencies and sold-out prosecutors have jumped on. (To reiterate, just because the police and/or reporting party do not LIKE what someone is doing, does not give either entity the authority to STOP what the person is doing. For whatever reason, oathbreakers seem incapable of getting this simple fact to sink into their addled brains.)

Suspicious or not, it is no one's business what a person is doing as long as they are not breaking the law. Seeing Tiny Tim tiptoeing through the tulips would look suspicious; however, being a weirdo who did something no one else did only made Tiny Tim an original thinker, not a criminal.

Would anyone care to venture a guess what would happen if someone called the police and an oathbreaker showed up, especially if the tulips Tiny Tim was seen tiptoeing through were within sight of a government facility? Tiny Tim would be tiptoed into the back of a police cruiser and tiptoed into a cage at the jail. His one phone call would be to his ex-wife, Miss Vicki, who would have to tiptoe her way down to the local pawnshop to sell Tiny Tim's ukulele in order to come up with the bond money.

None of this is rocket science. As a noted expert on the matter once asked me, "Who trained these officers?"

> "Who trained these officers?" - Don McCrea, subject-matter expert on the Fourth Amendment.

Point of fact is that in many of the nonconsensual encounters between a police officer and a suspicious person, the officer will freely admit there is no evidence to suggest that a crime was, is, or is about to be committed. One surefire indicator that an officer has absolutely no idea if an element of a crime is involved, is when the officer says, "I have absolutely no idea if an element of a crime is involved."

This leaves just one pathway open to justify either further detention or arrest: the person being detained must confess to a crime. Yet, like Tiny Tim, the so-called suspicious person may find themselves being shackled and thrown into a cage - without an admission of wrongdoing - for no reason other than a police officer or member of the public did not like (or did not understand) what the person was doing.

This is what happened to Mr. Patel, only he ended up with a broken neck out of the deal.

CHAPTER THIRTEEN

How to Make an Unlawful Detention

It's been more than 50 years since Terry v. Ohio. How is
it that so many police officers keep getting it wrong?

If there were ever a study involving basic incompetence in a law
enforcement officer, it would have to include Lexington, Kentucky
Police Officer D. McCue as one of its test subjects. To his credit
Officer McCue did not arrest the "suspicious person", although he
was headed down that path to be sure. Making a false arrest is merely
the byproduct of incompetence, not the cause of it. What makes the
encounter noteworthy is that McCue checked off most of the boxes
on the "how to butcher what should have been a consensual contact" checklist.

Officer McCue contacted a man who was passing out business cards in a residential neighborhood. It is unclear why McCue contacted the man in the first place; if he were responding to a suspicious person report, or whether he made contact while on routine patrol. Neither possibility relieved McCue of his responsibility to know the law and to respect the constitutional rights of a free human being.

What follows is a summary of McCue's most pertinent statements and actions from beginning to end, with the man's responses excluded due to time and space constraints. Let me just say that he stood his ground!

1. McCue first contacted the man on the sidewalk leading to a private residence. McCue made the international symbol for requesting ID (i.e. the proper spacing of index finger and thumb) and asked, "You got any ID on you?"

2. "Hang on one second for me. Hang on! You're being detained. You're being detained!" McCue physically restrained the man by grabbing hold of the man's left forearm. "Don't move. Don't move! Yes, you are (being detained)! We've had a lot of break-ins recently!" (if so, a happenstance of geography). "This is an investigation. We don't often have people walking up and down driveways. You aren't in any trouble. No, you're being detained! You're being detained!" (McCue had embarked upon a chartered deep-sea fishing expedition.)

> **"You aren't in any trouble. No, you're being detained!"**

3. McCue physically restrained the man a second time, again grabbing hold of the man's left forearm. "Stop walking away from me! Stop walking away from me!" He released the man's arm and reached for the mic clipped to his uniform shirt. McCue was making his first call for backup (classic displacement activity), which was clearly an unnecessary escalation.

4. To de-escalate an escalating contact, the man provided his name along with his business card. McCue followed the man down the street, at one point saying, "Quit

walking away from me. I'm telling you. I'm trying to work with you!"

5. "I need your date of birth!" (to run a warrant check). When the man reminded Officer McCue that he had committed no crime, McCue said, "Well, I don't know that!"

6. McCue denied causing the man any problems, except that he <u>had</u> caused the man problems by his unlawful detention. McCue again requested backup, which was another needless escalation. Nothing is more dangerous to an innocent person than the arrival of backup officers. Nothing. Plausible deniability is in play. This is the point where an incompetent oathbreaker is most likely to threaten arrest for "obstructing an investigation". This is also the point where an incompetent oathbreaker is most likely to ruin a life.

7. "I'm just trying to get a little bit of information. What is your date of birth? How about your (social security number)?" McCue was probably stalling for time, waiting for the arrival of the backup officer(s) to bail him out.

8. McCue said "Why not?" after the man again refused to provide any additional information. Rightly or wrongly, an oathbreaker will interpret the lack of cooperation as indicative of a guilty mind and use it to justify a probable cause arrest. Confess and go to jail; don't confess and go to jail, regardless, is not unheard of in the land of oathbreakers.

9. McCue made his third request for backup.

10. "I'm just talking with you. You're being ridiculous! You were walking up and down driveways; (no), it's not a crime. I'm trying to find out why you're walking up and down driveways!"

Officer McCue ended the unlawful detention and the young entrepreneur walked away. The backup officers McCue requested never appeared, which is probably the reason the man walked away instead of walking into a cage.

If my critique of Officer McCue's handling of the situation seems harsh, it is on purpose. McCue is not about to catch a break for his job-related incompetence. Incompetent people with guns and qualified immunity have no business patrolling the street, unencumbered by any semblance of proper oversight.

Trust the thin blue line? Hardly.

Pueblo, Colorado Police Department
On March 30, 2018, an activist was unlawfully detained and subsequently handcuffed by Officer Romero for filming the police station where Romero worked. This unconstitutional act by Officer Romero was an example of police "tribalism" and a manifestation of the disconnect between the citizens and police.

"You're being detained!"

Police "tribalism" is based on the assumption that everyone else is an imminent threat and that the police must band together in order to survive; therefore, the only person a police officer can trust is another member of the law enforcement "tribe". As a result, the constitutional rights of the citizens fade into the background - never to be seen again.

Of Romero's many foolish remarks, there was one that stood out among the rest: "I don't know what you're doing", which was Romero's way of saying "I don't LIKE what you're doing." It confirmed that Romero was on a fishing expedition in contradistinction to the requirements necessary to make a lawful detention.

It took the direct intervention of a knowledgeable and very professional Patrol Sergeant to set the activist free. On the other hand, Officer Romero's incompetence cost the City of Pueblo $41,000 for violating the activist's First Amendment right to record in public, and for violating his Fourth Amendment right to privacy. Not knowing what the activist was doing was the result of Officer Romero not knowing what he was doing, a case of poetic justice, perhaps?

Southlake, Texas Police Department

Whoever is responsible for search and seizure training at the Texas law enforcement academy needs to find another line of work, preferably one in a galaxy far, far away. In theory, an oathbreaker like Corporal B. Hernandez is supposed to receive training on the basics of search and seizure and pass a test. Hernandez did not pay attention, apparently.

Take a good look at the picture. In the distance, approximately 300 yards away, is a jet fuel storage facility. To the left is the insufferable Cpl. Hernandez, spinning a line of [expletive] to an activist about his filming the facility being "suspicious" (obviously because the activist was a committed terrorist, the kind who do target assessments in broad daylight — while standing alongside a heavily-traveled highway).

Cpl. Hernandez said he had "reasonable suspicion" and kept saying it to the point of becoming really annoying. Reasonable suspicion of what particular crime, genius? For taking photographs of round white tanks from 300 yards away? (See how easy it is for someone like Hernandez to substitute their prolific imagination for articulation? By the way, thanks for removing any doubt about what was stored inside the tanks, Cpl. Hernandez!)

Being a no-nonsense kind of oathbreaker, Hernandez hand-cuffed the activist and did a full-blown search of his person and backpack until he found the activist's identification. Anyone care to venture a guess what the insufferable Hernandez did next?

Corporal Hernandez should consider putting the kibosh on Google Street View for taking crystal clear, panoramic images of everything under the sun; images that are subsequently uploaded to the Internet. Or how about taking a run at Google Earth for upload-ing crystal clear satellite images that show the entire layout of the facility from above; images that can be zoomed in so closely, one can almost read what is on a person's mind?

To the cadre of trainers back at the academy, please be sure to scratch out the current search and seizure training outline and scribble in "Do whatever you want"; preferably before the next class of fresh-faced recruits arrives for indoctrination.

San Bernardino County, California Parole and Probation

In 2017, an incident between an activist and law enforcement may be one of the most infamous examples of how out of control domestic law enforcement has become since 9/11, along with the perceived uptick in violence against the police.

It all started on another glorious day in sunny southern California. An activist and his young son were strolling around the campus where the San Bernardino County Probation and Parole was headquartered. As the pair were about to depart the campus, they found themselves suddenly surrounded by a mob of no less than six (the number would soon grow to more than TWENTY) San Bernardino County Probation and Parole Officers.

Nearly every agent was sporting the latest trend in oathbreaker fashion wear: shaved heads, sunglasses, and military-style vests loaded with an array of military-style tactical gear. Both thumbs hooked inside their vests - reminiscent of the days when cops hooked their thumbs in their gun belts - accompanied by an appropriate level of hostility toward an American citizen and the ensemble was complete.

Probation Officer J. Holmes was one of the first to lay hands on the father by grabbing hold of a belt loop on the father's pants. "Hey! Look at me, everybody!" he probably thought. "I'm going to make us feel safer by holding onto this guy's belt loop!"

Officer J. "Haymaker" Holmes had unlawfully seized the father and violated both his First and Fourth Amendment rights in the process. In his rush to be a hero, Officer J. "You'd Better Have Deep Pockets" Holmes had just made the biggest mistake of his career, or what was left of it.

After two minutes of holding onto a fully-grown man's belt loop, and with his reputation at stake among his peers, Officer J. "In Way Over His Head" Holmes had to act. So he and several of his assumed-to-be-former colleagues took the father forcibly to the ground and placed him in handcuffs, while his son stood nearby watching.

Even if he had wanted to at this point, Officer J. "Hulk Hogan" Holmes had forfeited his chance to say to the activist Mea Culpa, which, loosely translated, means "I'm sorry!" in Latin. In the latest version of the world in which Probation Officer J. "Peach Picker"

Holmes found himself, his Mea Culpa moment meant finding a way to pay for his kid's college tuition from Debtors' Prison.

Los Angeles, California Police Department

An encounter between two activists and officers from the LAPD still manages to bring my Irish temper to the fore. The men were simply standing on the sidewalk filming an area police station and whatever else they could see in public. What bothered me most about the encounter was the officers' cavalier attitude and surreal sense of entitlement.

Understand that what the activists were doing was perfectly legal, which did not stop the officers from unlawfully detaining, handcuffing, and searching the men. One recurring statement was that the men had no legal right to film a police station, even if the men were filming from a public sidewalk.

No, it was the *officers*, not the activists, who had no legal "right" to stop the men from filming the police station from a public sidewalk. (Is there not even ONE, otherwise lawful activity that an oathbreaker won't attempt to criminalize, when done strictly to advance his or her best interest?) Unhelpful to the situation was the over-the-shoulder remark by a seething Corporal Peaks, who said as he slipped on his one-size-fits-all bin Laden kneepads, "You could be al-Qaeda terrorists for all we know!"

What a fool, too blinded by fear and loathing to understand the implications behind his remark. This is why the government and its obedient order-followers will always pose an existential threat to the safety and well-being of the Constitution.

How many LAPD officers did it take to violate the men's civil rights, perchance? Eleven. This was not about the LAPD officers being cautious. This was about the LAPD officers being cowards.

Joint Base Myer-Henderson Hall, Department of Defense: Arlington, Virginia

An activist seen filming the installation from a public sidewalk was soon approached by DOD Police Officer Daniel and unlawfully detained for "suspicious activity". Next came two MPs and the arrival of smug know-it-all, DOD Police Officer Lewis.

Smooth Operator Lewis

"Smooth Operator" Lewis took charge of the scene and began his methodical march towards tyranny. He went from one unconstitutional act to another, starting with a pat-down for weapons; ordering the activist to surrender his ID; placing him in handcuffs (as ordered by Staff Sergeant Hook); and forcing him to sit in the back of a police vehicle for an indeterminate period of time.

It was Detective Mitchell who eventually released the activist from custody. Simply put, the activist's constitutional rights had been shredded by the rights-robbing robots working on behalf of the Department of Defense.

Our military is a multibillion-dollar industry specializing in death and destruction, yet it had been brought to its knees by one man standing on a sidewalk holding a $300 camera. Oorah!

FBI: El Paso, Texas

For those who look upon government agencies like the Federal Bureau of Intimidation as being above reproach, think again. Only recently, an activist was mauled by a cadre of four FBI agents after he was spotted filming the exterior of the FBI Headquarters building from a public sidewalk.

For those who look upon government agencies like the Federal Bureau of Intimidation as being above reproach, think again.

Undisciplined and full of disdain, each agent played a role in stripping the activist of his constitutional rights. One agent grabbed hold and twisted the activist's wrist while the others seized his cameras, searched his person, and badgered him with open-ended accusations of being a terrorist sympathizer.

The four junior G-men called the El Paso Police Department and complained that the activist had used profanity during the altercation, which led to the activist being cited for disorderly conduct.

Gotta love how that works, a citizen being charged with disorderly conduct for hurting the feelings of federal agents, right after he had been roughed up and stripped of his rights by the same four federal agents. The thin blue line runs deep in El Paso.

Long gone are the days when the legendary junior G-men would hunt down violent gangsters toting Thompson submachine guns. Nowadays, the legendary junior G-men devote their massive resources to hunting down citizens toting a Canon˙.

FBI - America's Nomenklatura

This Gestapo-like behavior was not unexpected, seeing how the FBI considers itself to be the kingpins of law enforcement. FBI agents are at the top of the government food chain; an entitlement that allows them to engage in extra-legal pursuits, such as assaulting an American citizen engaged in a constitutionally protected activity.

A quick search of twentieth-century history reveals the same extra-legal mindset existed among members of the nomenklatura, or ruling class of the former Soviet Union. Its entitled members enjoyed Pule cheese, Beluga caviar, and Dom Pérignon Champagne; whereas the workers enjoyed spoiled leftovers and watered-down vodka.

How the nomenklatura at the FBI found time to strip an American citizen of his constitutional rights is anyone's guess. My impression was they were too busy planning another soft coup to take down the American electoral process, as well as trying to unseat a duly-elected President.

Pima County, Arizona Sheriff's Department

Three activists were quietly filming from inside the public lobby at the Pima County Courthouse. No sooner had they walked outside when they were arrested, charged with the "crime" of violating the privacy rights of the citizens inside the lobby. Where to begin?

It is not the actions of citizens that are constrained by the Fourth Amendment to the Constitution, but the actions of the government. Furthermore, it is not the responsibility of state and local governments to investigate civil rights violations. That is the responsibility of the Federal Bureau of Intimidation on behalf of the Department of Injustice.

These arrests were strictly retaliatory in nature, most likely approved by the faceless and feckless tyrants in upper-level management. The charges were so outrageous that, for all intents and purposes, the activists might as well have been arrested for inhaling and exhaling.

FBI and Baton Rouge, Louisiana Police Department

Neither of the two corrupt FBI agents had to do the heavy lifting, not when they had a corrupt Baton Rouge police detective to do the heavy lifting for them. The detective, serving as a liaison officer with the FBI, had confronted an activist seen filming the facility from a public sidewalk some distance away.

The detective demanded ID, grabbed the activist's elbow, and forced him to splay out over the hood of the detective's pickup truck. Without so much as reasonable suspicion of a crime, the detective rifled through the activist's pockets until he located the man's billfold. It was all perfunctory after that.

With the activist still splayed out over the hood of the pickup, the detective had the audacity to say that he had not deprived the activist of his constitutional rights. All the while stood the two pretentious and unidentified FBI agents, smirking with arms folded, thoroughly enjoying the "tour de force" of their comrade.

FBI: Mobile, Alabama

An activist was taking pictures of the FBI Field Office from a public sidewalk when out of the fortified compound marched four armed FBI agents, determined to find out who had the audacity to take a picture of the King's castle.

They first surrounded, then tried to coerce the activist into surrendering his ID. "You're taking pictures of where we work," the agent in charge of the field interview said, "and that makes us kinda nervous." To his credit, the activist held firm and refused to identify himself.

Despite being trained investigators, there was one minor detail the agents had overlooked: their very own website displays images of the building where the FBI Field Office is located.

Then, in 2019, it happened again. A different activist was approached by three Mobile police officers and ordered to surrender his ID. Even though he was an experienced activist, the man had made the mistake of smoking in public. This led to a ticket and the necessity of surrendering his ID.

FBI and Marion, Illinois Police Department

"Hey, you do realize that if someone comes out here and says that you're alarming them by filming them, you can be charged with disorderly conduct?" Patrol Officer Ward said to three activists whom he had detained for filming the local FBI Field Office.

Ward and a second officer had responded to a frantic 911 call placed by one of the most obnoxious FBI agents on the planet, who was just clever enough to play off of Ward's admonishment. "I'm telling you officer, and I'm telling them, I feel alarmed that they're filming my building without identifying who they are."

Now no longer detained, the men were walking away when Marion Police Sergeant "Lurch" showed up - without a shred of objectivity. "So here's the deal," the big galoot started in on the men, "we have a victim of disorderly conduct. Someone at the FBI Office was alarmed and disturbed by your behavior. So, at this point, y'all are under arrest." Click! Click! Click!

Sgt. "Lurch"

Their arrest for disorderly conduct was only a ruse to force the activists to identify themselves. This was for the sole benefit of agente federal Obnoxious, who had every intention of shipping their personal information on over to the local Fusion Center for inclusion on the government's Terrorist Watchlist.

To the chagrin of the oathbreakers, not one of the activists surrendered their identification while in police custody. It was the local prosecutor who finally set things straight with the arresting officers, including Sergeant Lurch. Lacking a victim, she refused to prosecute on the charge of disorderly conduct and sternly ordered the officers to return the men to the place where they had been arrested.

This is what an honest prosecutor is supposed to do when oathbreakers make a false arrest. As demonstrated, this is the reason why I tend to blame prosecutors when the justice system falls apart. Thanks to a prosecutor honoring their oath, an injustice was averted and real justice prevailed.

An obnoxious, self-entitled FBI agent said the word "alarmed" and three obedient oathbreakers from the Marion, Illinois Police

Department jumped. One entity of the government had called upon another entity of the government to dispose of something the first entity of the government did not like. See how that works?

Springfield, Oregon Police Department

If the community of oathbreakers were to pick just one of its members to be a poster child for ignorant abuse of authority, it would have to be Sergeant Rick Lewis. Sergeant Lewis went hands-on with an activist within seconds of making contact. In the mind of an oathbreaker like Lewis, passively filming a government building rises to the level of disorderly conduct.

King Lewis the Lionhearted stacked an additional charge of criminal trespass on the activist, even though the activist was standing on public property at the time. Although both charges were later dismissed, the question remains why the cases had gone as far as they did?

It was an unlawful detention that quickly melded into an unlawful arrest, because Lewis said that the activist's presence made him feel "nervous". So, too, were the other heavily-armed and gargantuan police officers similarly "nervous". Cowardice couched behind an insubstantial claim of "officer safety" has, in the mind of an oathbreaker like Lewis, replaced probable cause as the legal standard to arrest. All that remains is a manufactured crime.

Plantation, Florida Police Department

Meet Plantation Police Officer J. Quaregna, or "Q" for short. "Q" is "one of those officers" whose tiny brain landed on the floor with a splat! the moment they pinned on their shiny new badge and first wore their trick or treat clown costume.

"Q"

In January 2019, Q accosted an independent journalist for taking pictures of Plantation General Hospital from the outside. Q's threatening and unprofessional behavior has to be seen to be believed: crazy in the head; barking orders at the journalist to stop filming and delete the video; babbling; threatening arrest; and completely out of control.

When the journalist balked, Q went straight to his portable radio and called for backup. Gathering the gang to save their bacon is what oathbreakers do when they are unsure what to do next.

Four more clowns from the Plantation Police Department showed up. That made for a total of five clowns, three security guards, one nurse, and at least one hospital administrator. All this manic activity over one man taking pictures of a hospital, in a country formerly known as America.

"You're breaking the HIPAA Law!" two of the clowns honked incessantly. HIPAA, short for the "Hospital Insurance Portability and Accountability Act" passed by Congress during the Clinton

Administration. What does the Act do? Well, it has nothing to do with taking pictures of a hospital.

Undeterred and on a mission, the clowns handcuffed the journalist on suspicion of violating HIPAA - the Act that has nothing to do with taking pictures of a hospital - and performed a pat-down for weapons. Something the clowns overlooked was that they lacked the jurisdiction to enforce federal laws.

There we have it, folks. American law enforcement at its best and finest. In this case, it was a group of five clowns led by Q, the first clown to step from the clown car determined to make an arrest.

Glynn County, Georgia Sheriff's Department

George Washington wrote centuries-ago the following: "Government is not reason; it is not eloquence; it is force! Like fire, it is a dangerous servant and a fearful master." His words were an explicit warning to America's citizens then - and to all who would follow.

If Washington were alive today, he would no doubt be deeply troubled by the rights-robbing behavior of American law enforcement. Washington might even compare their behavior to that of Hessian soldiers during the Revolutionary War.

With thoughts of the insufferable conditions his soldiers endured at Valley Forge, Washington would surely cry out in his loudest voice "Lobster Backs!" upon hearing the news of what transpired between an activist and two tyrannical jail administrators from Glynn County, Georgia.

Dumb and Dumber

The activist was filming the Glynn County Courthouse and nearby Sheriff's Office from across the street when he was suddenly set upon by a county jail administrator. With the rapidity of a machine gun, the man demanded to see the activist's ID. He unexpectedly tore the camera from the activist's grasp, returned it, then tore the camera from the activist's grasp a second time.

A second jail administrator showed up who, like the ever-helpful first administrator, repeatedly threatened the activist with violence. "We're about to have us a problem!" he ranted. "I'm fixin' to take you to jail if'n you don't stop filming!" More threats of violence quickly followed, with the second administrator yelling, "I can, and I will, put you in jail!"

Precisely what crime had the activist committed that nearly got him beaten up and thrown into a cage like an animal? His "crime" was taking photographs of the courthouse at the same time as several shackled prisoners were being perp-walked from the jail to the courthouse. Prisoners who, like everyone else, have ZERO expectation of privacy while in public.

It is unimaginable to think that the activist was being threatened with violence when it was the same two thick-headed jail administrators who paraded the prisoners outside for the world to see to begin with. These are the very same government workers who post images of the prisoners on a publicly-accessible website, then announce to the world that some of the prisoners are convicted sex offenders. What am I missing here?

The County Sheriff eventually arrived and, using a far more reasoned approach, fielded the activist's harassment complaint against his two oafish jail administrators. In the end, the Sheriff agreed to provide his staff with updated training on the issue of public photography.

A couple of farm-fresh idiots working on behalf of the government had treated the activist no differently than if he were a prisoner himself. What were they thinking, or were they?

Sacramento, California Police Department

Patrol Officer Frazier (badge #423) of the Sacramento Police Department is more than an incompetent oathbreaker. Officer Frazier has the honor of being a dangerously incompetent oathbreaker. No police officer has the authority to simply walk up to someone not breaking the law - a photographer, in this case - and use a pain compliance technique to force them to the ground for handcuffing. Both the detention as well as Frazier's use of force were unlawful and unconstitutional.

Yet law enforcement is replete with officers like Frazier. For sure they are cowards, desiring to "hook everyone up" when they arrive on the scene of a call for fear of the unknown. No, they do NOT get to hide behind a smokescreen of "officer safety!" as the reason to deny a citizen their constitutional rights, let alone use unreasonable force to subdue someone who poses no threat. Then, afterward, to stand around laughing and playing grab a** with their fellow oathbreakers.

What a disgrace, the way innocent citizens are being pummeled by law enforcement for engaging in a constitutionally protected activity like public photography. A bigger disgrace is the whiney sailors and Marines at the U.S. Naval and Marine Corps Center who called the police in the first place.

Pevely, Missouri Police Department

An activist was filming a nighttime traffic stop from some 200 feet away when Officer Wayne Casey left the scene of the stop, drove to where the man was quietly standing, and threatened to arrest him for interfering with Casey's traffic stop - even though there were plenty of other officers helping Casey with the stop.

Just in case the reader is a cop from Pevely, Missouri, or Leon Valley, Texas, I'll write slower, with emphasis on the really important parts: an activist was filming a nighttime traffic stop from some 200 FEET AWAY when Officer Wayne Casey LEFT THE SCENE OF THE STOP, drove to where the man was quietly standing, and threatened to arrest him for INTERFERING WITH CASEY'S TRAFFIC STOP...

Casey made the preposterous claim that the activist's presence had diverted his attention from the stop to keep an eye on the activist. He must have missed seeing the 80,000-pound semis passing by his stop an arms-length away. Casey even managed to invoke a phantom officer safety claim when he yelled, "DO YOU KNOW HOW FAR A RIFLE CAN SHOOT?"

If Casey intended to overwhelm the activist with his unique style of ceaseless babbling, it worked. He surrendered his ID and promptly left the area.

In hindsight, it was fortunate the activist chose not to challenge Casey the night he was harassed. Casey and a fellow officer were soon fired for an unrelated event involving the violent assault of an inmate at the jail, which Casey witnessed but failed to intervene. Casey also failed to report the assault to upper-level management, despite the incident being caught on a jail surveillance camera.

Colorado Springs, Colorado Police Department

An activist observed filming a police substation was detained and placed into the back of a police car, accused of "disorderly conduct" by Sergeant Brad Pratt and Patrol Officer Steve Pugsley. Before he was placed in chains, the activist was told that suspicious activity was a misdemeanor offense. What oathbreakers will say or do to make an unconstitutional arrest is remarkable.

Airport Police: Tampa, Florida International Airport

A father and his 13-year-old son were filming airplanes taking off - silhouetted by a beautiful sunset - from a public sidewalk when they were unlawfully detained by Officer Finley. An unprofessional Officer Finley went through the usual list of "infractions" that have become the norm in post-9/11 America: trespassing citizens from PUBLIC property; and filming without prior authorization from the government.

What Officer Finley and other oathbreakers are missing is obvious, which is that anyone can stand on adjacent private property and lawfully take pictures of airplanes taking off and landing. Officer Finley attempted to criminalize the filming of airplanes; not because of the physical act of filming, per se, but more so because of where the father and son were standing at the time they were filming.

This story does not end with Officer Finley's attempt to criminalize a constitutionally protected activity. Soon after the confrontation, the father received a phone call at home from Airport Chief of Police Paul F. Sireci. What made Chief Sireci's phone call so noteworthy was that he had called not to say "or else", but to say "I'm sorry." Will oathbreakers pay attention?

CHAPTER FOURTEEN

America's Ever-Growing "You Can't Do That!" Mentality

Those who still believe that America is the land of the free have not been keeping up with current events.

9/11 (and now the coronavirus) fundamentally, and likely permanently, transformed America from a resolute "can do" nation into an irresolute "can't do" nation, where even the most rudimentary parts of American life are now considered a threat to national security. It is a sad and pathetic state-of-affairs when citizens and law enforcement officers alike know only how to start a sentence with "YOU CAN'T DO THAT!" because, whatever it is, it is presumed to be illegal, even when it is not. Chronic naysaying has replaced baseball as America's newest national sport.

A citizen's knee-jerk, "You can't do that!" reaction is usually in response to something they see but don't understand; if they don't understand what they see, chances are they won't like what they see. If they don't like what they see, chances are the police will show up. If the police show up, chances are someone will go to jail.

Like citizens, a police officer's knee-jerk "You can't do that!" reaction is also in response to something they see but don't like, such as being filmed in the performance of their duties or seeing someone filming one of their precious buildings. If the police show up under those circumstances, chances are someone will go to jail.

At the center of the "You can't do that!" universe is the government, the omnipotent and unfathomable creature that sends out its armed order-followers to enforce the master's "You can't do that!" edicts. These are the men and women of law enforcement, the ones who set aside their intellect in exchange for a fat paycheck and top-notch healthcare benefits.

Still unconvinced about the government's longstanding role in denying fundamental human rights and suppressing freedom? How about we use American history as a neutral observer?

Voter disenfranchisement and the tenets of institutional-ized racism were work products of the GOVERNMENT. It was the GOVERNMENT that enacted "Black codes" and disparaging Jim Crow laws, legal abominations meant to further deny African-Americans their most basic human rights. Passage of the Indian Removal Act in 1830 led to the infamous "Trail of Tears" and the death of 4,000 Native Peoples. Did even one go to their doom voluntarily?

J. Edgar Hoover, the "Bull Connor" of American law enforce-ment, used his unparalleled power as the longstanding FBI Director (1935-1972) to spy on American citizens whom he deemed were "enemies of the state" - primarily civil rights activists, including Dr. Martin Luther King. Dr. King was, according to Hoover, "The most dangerous Negro in the future of this nation."

Hoover was well-suited for the job of FBI Director. In 1919, Hoover, as leader of the General Intelligence Division, was instru-mental in carrying out the little-known "Palmer Raids", where federal agents conducted raids without search warrants and arrested, then deported, hundreds of suspected "subversives" without due process.

In 1956, Director Hoover, having grown frustrated with the limitations placed on his investigative efforts, created the Counter Intelligence Program, or COINTELPRO. Its select membership conducted a series of covert, and oftentimes unconstitutional, investigations designed to discredit political opponents, subversives, and other known "deviants".

By 1960, the FBI had open files on 432,000 Americans, files Director Hoover kept locked away in his office in Washington D.C. Whatever his accomplishments, and there were many, Hoover's legacy is tarnished by his unconstitutional abuse of authority; his desire to use that power to violate civil liberties for the sake of national security.

This is not a political or ideological manifesto. Nor is it intended to discredit the work of federal law enforcement agencies as a whole, although they certainly deserve it. This is about how it took only ONE AGENT OF THE GOVERNMENT to subvert the Constitution and do so with absolute impunity.

Yet, as of this writing, more and more Americans are running helter-skelter TOWARD the government, rather than running AWAY from the government. These are the two-legged variety of lemmings - the kind that look forward to jumping from cliffs - who truly believe that one day soon, an agent of government will guide them into the Promised Land.

Placing full faith and credit in the government is hazardous to liberty for the simple reason that government's "solution" to a perceived problem is to enact more laws that further restrict freedom. Practicality notwithstanding, what is the government's solution to end so-called "gun violence"? Repeal the Second Amendment* and turn millions of Americans into unindicted felons.

Does someone have a differing political or ideological opinion? Restrict freedom of speech, a truly vicious and uncompromising movement that has taken root on college campuses. The truth is that America is undergoing an insidious contraction of rights, rights that are no longer being honored by the government; none of which could happen were it not for the obedient order-followers in law enforcement.

> **The truth is that America is undergoing an insidious contraction of rights, rights that are no longer being honored by the government...**

Unlike laws enacted by the government, nothing in the Constitution forces anyone to do anything against their will. For example, the Second Amendment does not force anyone to own a firearm. It simply acknowledges the fact that every human being has the inherent right to self-protection. This holds true for every other right enumerated in the Constitution. They are available, if and when a citizen chooses to exercise the right.

To repeal or diminish any of the amendments is foolish and most likely irreversible. Remember that, before mailing a check to one of America's thousands of self-absorbed, freedom-killing "You can't do that!" organizations.

*States have begun to enact so-called "red flag" laws in response to a number of high-profile shootings. These laws are intended to be enforced proactively, without the benefit of due process, by granting law enforcement and family members the authority to petition for the temporary removal of firearms from a person arbitrarily deemed to be a threat to others. Overzealous enforcement and malicious prosecutions will be the inevitable byproducts of red flag laws. In fact, it has already started.

CHAPTER FIFTEEN

Policing Freedom of Speech

Police officers who police free speech are [expletive] tyrants.

Benjamin Franklin famously said, "Those who can give up essential liberty to obtain a little temporary safety deserve neither liberty nor safety." Accordingly, citizens who choose safety over liberty are much more likely to be ignorant of the Constitution, generally; and their constitutional rights, specifically. They become like sheep in a pen, guarded by 900,000 ravenous wolves.

> Our Founding Fathers recognized that rights are fleeting; that to defend one's rights, one must first know their rights.

Our Founding Fathers recognized that rights are fleeting; that to defend one's rights, one must first know their rights. Where this process begins is knowing that not every clause in the Constitution is meant to shackle the authority of the government. On the contrary, much of the Constitution is about establishing general principles of self-governance and the laying out of legal principles and protocols. To learn more about the Constitution and how it protects citizens from government overreach, look no further than the first ten Amendments - appropriately named the "Bill of Rights".

Of the ten amendments listed in the Bill of Rights, there are three that serve a pivotal role in reining in the government: the First ("Congress shall make no law"); Second ("shall not be infringed"); and Fourth ("shall not be violated"). Unfortunately, many Americans are unfamiliar with these amendments and their respective provisions.

What I find incomprehensible is knowing that millions of Americans are actively campaigning to strip themselves and their fellow citizens of these rights. Sadly, at the same time as America is tearing apart the Constitution, other nations are embracing its precepts and are using it as a model in their quest for freedom.

Because the Constitution is inherently skeptical of the government, it makes sense that it would cast a skeptical eye towards the origin of the rights enumerated therein. Anchoring the Constitution is the novel idea that rights do not originate from the government, but from nature's law. "Rights" that originate from the government are "rights" that the government can take away. The government governs clumsily and will steal the rights of citizens if it serves a purpose.

Bill of Rights

Amendment 1 U.S. citizens have freedom of religion, speech, press, assembly, and petition.

Amendment 2 U.S. citizens have the right to keep and bear arms, or own guns.

Amendment 3 The government may not force U.S. citizens to shelter soldiers in their homes.

Amendment 4 U.S. citizens are protected from unreasonable searches of a person's property.

Amendment 5 The government may not force U.S. citizens to testify against themselves in court.

Amendment 6 U.S. citizens have the right to a fair and speedy trial.

Amendment 7 U.S. citizens have the right to a trial by jury.

Amendment 8 U.S. citizens are protected from cruel and unusual punishment.

Amendment 9 U.S. citizens may have rights that are not listed in the Constitution.

Amendment 10 Powers not given to the federal government by the U.S. Constitution belong to the state or to the people.

True rights can never be taken away, as they are seen as an upwelling of natural rights such as life and liberty that live in the heart of a free human being. In terms of the government's role and the Constitution, it has no role other than to oversee the amendment process and protect the rights of citizens.

This essential fact is meant to shield citizens from the excesses of a tyrannical government, something every law enforcement officer is supposed to know BEFORE they hit the street. A cadet who graduated from their respective law enforcement training academy ignorant of this underlying principle must have either slept through the training or cheated on the test.

Laws are what constrain the actions of citizens (i.e. "No person shall"), which must be written in conformity with the limits outlined in the Constitution. These limits recognize that civil rights are both unassailable and unalienable, as no person may hold a lien or bond against them.

Put yet another way, the Constitution protects citizens from the government, the government enacts laws to protect the citizens, and law enforcement enforces the laws enacted by the government on behalf of the citizens.

This is how the government is supposed to interact with citizens and why armed agents of the government are called "law enforcement officers". It is NEVER the job of a police officer to enforce thoughts, feelings, concerns, mere suspicions, simple gestures, whatifs, or imaginary speech codes.

Yet it is happening, especially in regard to free speech. Citizens engaged in a constitutionally protected activity, such as free speech, are rotting away in jail because someone with a badge thought their job description included being the arbiter of America's mores and norms. Worse is how willing these tyrants take to the job.

Along with other rights, oathbreakers, in collaboration with certain left-leaning political elements, are chipping away at free speech in America. Their efforts so far appear to be working.

South Tucson, Arizona Police Department

An activist was chained and caged for disorderly conduct after an officer solicited a bystander to say they were "bothered" by the man's language. The man must have seen his life flash before his eyes when he saw the two officers walk up. One, clearly a military veteran, had so many tattoos on his arms it looked like he was wearing a long sleeve shirt. A life-size Rorschach test. Not a good thing to see, as it usually precedes handcuffs and being thrown into a cage - as it did in South Tucson.

The University of North Carolina at Chapel Hill Police Department

A shout out to former Patrol Officer Annie Boone. Officer Boone stopped and detained a male driver for the crime of "indignity to a police officer" after she heard the Ph.D. student say "oink oink" in passing.

Boone even went so far as to issue a "code yellow" over her portable radio, then used the sudden assemblage of fellow officers to force the student into handing over his driver's license.

How pathetic. One can only imagine the level of violence that would have ensued had the student bid Officer Boone a good day and attempted to drive away.

Colorado Springs, Colorado Police Department

During a clearly retaliatory arrest for alleged jaywalking, Patrol Officer Matt Anderson aggressively approached and manhandled a citizen for flipping him the bird. Anderson had called for backup before he had even contacted the man, intentionally escalating the situation by telling officers the man was being "froggy", or otherwise uncooperative.

Next came the ubiquitous sound of approaching police sirens as five Colorado Springs police officers responded to Anderson's shameful request for help. Six heavily-armed and angry oathbreakers quickly descended upon an American citizen, for no other reason than the citizen had dared challenge the iron-fisted authority of the thin blue line.

Over what? For simply extending a middle finger, where the only "victim" was Anderson's fragile ego? Even if this were an isolated incident, it would still be problematic; however, there are far too many citizens who can attest that it is *anything* but an isolated incident. This is repulsive police behavior and it needs to stop.

What about the jaywalking infraction? Surely it needed to be addressed, *because walking across the street in the United States of America will not, and cannot, be tolerated!* Except, the crosswalk that Anderson claimed the man failed to use was three blocks away.

Comal County, Texas Sheriff's Department

A motorist was pulled over by two Comal County Sheriff's Deputies and threatened with arrest for disorderly conduct after having flipped the bird to the deputies. Being gum-chomping Puritans with a disdain for free speech and the Constitution are par for the course for Comal County Sheriff's Deputies.

Kentucky State Police

An Honorable Mention goes to Officer M. Dennis of the Kentucky State Police, who stopped a driver for the crime of hurting the officer's feelings. It seems Kentucky is a lot like Colorado and Texas, where drivers can be stopped and verbally harangued for flipping the bird to a police officer.

After pulling the man over and demanding to see his driver's license, a verbally-combative and seemingly unstable Dennis ordered the driver not to film the encounter. He then threatened to arrest the driver for the "crime" of "disrespecting the law". What the driver was failing to comprehend is that Kentucky State Trooper M. Dennis was in full meltdown mode.

Foolishly, the driver hurled an insult at Dennis as the trooper walked back to his cruiser. Trooper Dennis turned on his heels and marched right back to the car, where he angrily challenged the driver to say one more disparaging word.

"Act up again and I'm going to pull you out of this car!" Dennis shouted. "You'll be taken to jail for disorderly and menacing!" After one more testy exchange, the driver left, which was undoubtedly the wisest decision the man had made at that point in his life.

Columbia County, Florida Sheriff's Department
Sheriff's Deputy Travis English - who himself has a rather lengthy military and civilian criminal history - arrested a motorist for having a sticker in the rear window of his pickup, one whose message English found offensive. It read "I EAT ('DONKEY')" in big white letters.

A prudish English had enough sense to cover his pompous backside by contacting a patrol sergeant before making the arrest. "Arrest him, take him to jail, and tow his [expletive]," the Sergeant told English. Not much room for ambiguity in that answer!

Deputy High and Mighty arrested the linguistic terrorist and booked him into jail for "possessing obscene material" and "resisting without violence", the latter charge because the man refused to remove a letter from the naughty word.

"Resisting without violence" was intended for situations involving "passive resistance". An example would be peaceful protesters who lock arms and refuse to leave an area after repeated warnings. English used the law to throw the man into a cage for failing to heed the Eleventh Commandment, which was for not respecting English's made-up authority as a deeply-moral police officer.

Yet, not all of the blame can be placed on Deputy English. The real culprits are the politicians. Each time a governing body passes a law making it easier for the police to make an arrest, this is the result.

Travis English is an oathbreaker, one whose law enforcement philosophy is modeled after the rotund bloviator, Eric "Respect My Authoritah!" Cartman, from South Park. Sadly, whereas law enforcement was once under the thumb of FBI Director J. Edgar Hoover, it is now under the thumb of Deputy Travis English.

Carey, Ohio Police Department

May 14, 2019, was a picture-perfect day in Carey, Ohio. So much so that a young couple decided to go for a walk with their newborn baby and a friendly family pet. Working that afternoon was Patrol Officer Joshua Snyder who, to his credit, waved at the couple from the comfort of his cruiser as the foursome walked by. Their decision to go for a stroll that picture-perfect day was about to turn surreal when Officer Snyder rolled up, angered by the father's lack of civility.

Officer Snyder did not appreciate his thoughtful gesture being reciprocated with a middle-finger-only salute. Simply pointing at the clouds with the tip of a middle finger got the father thrown into a cage for disorderly conduct. "People are walking around, man!" Snyder whined as he pointed to some distant house. "People and little kids! That's disorderly conduct, man!" Snyder whined again. How ironic, since some of those same "little kids" will spend the rest of the day listening to Dad cuss outright like a drunken sailor; all the while killing cops in the highly-popular video game, "Grand Theft Auto".

Even worse than Snyder's whining and feigned indignation was the on-scene lieutenant blessed the arrest, as did the chief of police. It made no difference to Snyder that his grotesque behavior was captured for posterity on at least two cameras, one being his body camera. He lied in the arrest report, anyway.

A few days later, the man walked into the police station and asked Officer Chad Kessler for a complaint form. Kessler threatened to arrest the man and forced him to leave the property. What was the "crime" Kessler referred to? Disorderly conduct!

Fort Pierce, Florida Police Department

A civil rights advocate was standing on a sidewalk holding a sign that read "[EXPLETIVE] CITY HALL". This prompted someone to call 911. Recently-promoted Sergeant Christine Davis and at least three other Fort Pierce police officers responded to the call.

While speaking with the advocate, Sergeant Davis could not have sounded more serious than if she were a beach master trying to maintain some semblance of order on the beaches of Normandy. In a monotone voice, Davis droned on about how the advocate was legally required to answer her questions; his sign was providing "vulgar messages"; the First Amendment did not give him the right to use profanity and offend people; he was being uncooperative and giving her a bad time; he would be arrested for trespass if he did not leave the venue immediately; he could come back but only if he did not offend people; and that he would be arrested if he held up the sign again.

After the advocate had left the immediate area, Davis instructed her officers that the sidewalk was made for walking; therefore, the advocate could not "stay in one place". As Davis and her obedient comrades all nodded their heads in agreement, the sound of rocks bouncing around the inside of a tin can could be heard all the way to Pyongyang.

Royse City, Texas Police Department

Someone is driving along on a sunny day in Texas when they see a man holding one of three homemade signs. The man is standing in a road ditch and not bothering a soul. "Hmm," the driver thinks, "I wonder what's on the sign he's holding?" The driver gets closer and closer until, finally, he is close enough to read what is on the man's sign.

"911, what is your emergency?" "A man is holding a sign that offends me! Please hurry!" Just like that, three badge-toting arbiters of free speech arrived. Lickety-split, one of the badge-toting arbiters angrily tore the signs from the quiet man's hands. Off to a rancid cage he went after being arrested for disorderly conduct, resisting arrest, failure to ID, and interference with public duties. One year after his arrest, local prosecutors are still pursuing the charges.

The quiet man's constitutional rights had simply vanished, as if they had never existed. Courtesy of three sworn "defenders of the Constitution" and at least one easily-offended motorist. Sergeant Christine Davis would have surely nodded her head in agreement!

What was the message on the sign the quiet man was holding at the time of his arrest, by the way? The message read, "Give me liberty or give me death".

Sheboygan, Wisconsin Police Department

What would the world do without police officers like Michael McCarthy? McCarthy is a "chatterbox cop", one who tries to over-whelm people with an uninterrupted stream of blah blah baby-bab-bling. A "chatterbox cop" has the critical thinking skills on par with Gilligan, the brain-dead wannabe sailor from the 1960's TV sitcom, Gilligan's Island.

Then again, what would the world be like without Eric "Gilligan" Turner?

Turner's delusional world collided with that of an activist outside of a Sheboygan Post Office. The activist was doing a narrative about the Post Office and not bothering a soul when he was approached by an agitated Turner. He would not leave the activist alone, at one point saying, "Are you a terrorist? Are you plotting something?"

Turner called 911 to report he was being harassed by the activist. This made Turner the "First Caller". "First Callers" are the first to call the police during a dispute, which gives them an immediate advantage over the other party. Police will almost always interview the First Caller first to get their side of the story. Nine times out of ten, a First Caller will embellish the tale they tell the police. Worse, nine out of ten cops will believe the First Caller's story without hesitation.

Earlier, the activist had called Turner a "[expletive] idiot." This was in response to Turner's constant harassment, which included threats to smash the activist's camera. Officer McCarthy chose to focus his attention solely on the activist. "If I...ask (Turner) if he was offended by you calling him a [expletive] idiot, and he says 'yes," McCarthy started in with his blah blah baby-babbling, "you can be cited for disorderly conduct!"

Stirred into McCarthy's rapid-fire mix of crazy talk was something I had not heard since the first grade. An overly-excited McCarthy said, "You stood out here and called each other names!"

Once upon a time in kiddie land, name-calling meant a trip to the woodshed or Principal's Office. In Sheboygan, Wisconsin, name-calling between grownups meant the activist was arrested for disorderly conduct. Osama bin Laden's homeboy, Eric Turner, was allowed to simply walk away.

Kudos to Sheboygan, Wisconsin Patrol Officer Michael "Gilligan" McCarthy, whose arrest of the activist for name-calling ended worldwide poverty and led to wholesale nuclear disarmament! You, sir, are a [expletive] idiot.

Sherwood, Arkansas Police Department

A noise complaint brought an on-duty Sherwood Police Officer and an off-duty Pulasky County Sheriff's Deputy together in an encounter that left the deputy bloodied, arrested on three charges, and ultimately fired. It was yet another example of a police officer who was willing to use violence over free speech.

At the time he approached the deputy, the area was quiet and orderly. Other than making small talk and asking a few routine questions, the officer could have simply left. That is not how the world works in the mind of an oathbreaker.

In this case, the officer asked a series of increasingly personal questions such as the deputy's name and phone number. When the deputy hesitated, the officer claimed he needed the information under the orders of his sergeant. This is where the contact went off the rails.

The deputy had been drinking beforehand and was in no mood to entertain the officer's questions. When the officer persisted, the deputy used a term that disparaged the maternal side of the officer's breeding and ancestry.

His insult prompted a warning; there were children nearby, the officer intimated. One more profane word and the deputy would be arrested. The deputy said one more profane word and the officer kept his promise. Violence ensued because, as we all know, violence is what makes the world a safer place to live. It is certainly a better alternative than using profanity.

Handcuffed and bleeding from the head, the deputy was charged with disorderly conduct, resisting arrest, and public intoxication. Disorderly conduct for swearing, and resisting arrest for being disorderly because of swearing, but public intoxication? The deputy was on private property when he was arrested.

Using oathbreaker logic, that would technically make it a crime to be drunk anywhere in Sherwood, Arkansas. Which would also make it a crime to cuss anywhere in Sherwood, Arkansas. This means that in Sherwood, Arkansas, it is against the law to cuss, be drunk, or be drunk and cuss.

Moultrie, Georgia Police Department

On the day before Independence Day 2019, a civil rights advocate was chained and thrown into a cage after he was approached first by City Manager Peter Dillard, then by three city patrol officers. The advocate's "crime" and subsequent arrest for disorderly conduct was precipitated by the sign the activist was holding, as well as his failure to get a permit to protest. "You can do it the right way or we'll do it our way!" one of the oathbreakers chided during the arrest.

A second oathbreaker was kind enough to share his personal opinion on the matter. He said that, although he did not personally have a problem with the advocate exercising his First Amendment right to free speech, the advocate could not use language that offended someone. More offensive words were never spoken by a lawman, Officer Butterbean.

This simplistic view of the world gives further credence to the "heckler's veto" by encouraging malcontents to claim offense at the opinions of those with whom they disagree. Brilliant! Oathbreakers who believe their duties include policing the English language would be better suited working on America's college campuses, where free speech is on life support. Who would be better suited to apply the coup de grâce than an oathbreaker?

Incidentally, where might one find the list of "naughty" words, the ones that can never see the light of day in Moultrie, Georgia? Without an official list, the determination of what is or is not a naughty word would be left up to the discretion of the officers. Or are we to trust the wisdom and insight of government workers to decide for us?

Accolades continue to pour in for Peter Dillard and his Three Shortsighted Mice. All four worked hand-in-hand to keep their fellow "Moultrians" safe from being offended. In particular, for the proper way to protest, which is to apply for a permit to protest the very same people who would approve the permit to protest in the first place!

Because of four highly-offensive oathbreakers from the small southern town of Moultrie, Georgia, the now-familiar phrase embedded in the advocate's homemade sign had been validated: "[EXPLETIVE] CITY HALL".

Fort Worth, Texas Police Department (FWPD)

Note the contemptuous expressions chiseled into the faces of two oathbreakers from the FWPD. Polite professionalism is nowhere on their radar. This is the look one would expect to see from oathbreakers who show up in ARREST! mode, having already resolved to throw someone into a cage no matter the circumstances.

That is what these oathbreakers did after responding to a 911 call involving two men, one of whom took offense at being called an ***hole. What transpired after the officers' arrival is indicative of just how far this country has fallen, in terms of rugged individualism and the right to disagree without interference from the nanny state.

In present-day America, calling someone an ***hole means being taken to the ground under the threat of violence, handcuffed, and spending the night rotting inside a steel cage on a charge of disorderly conduct. Neither of these maleficent oathbreakers have any sense of the role they played in killing freedom. None at all.

Law enforcement is not the solution to every problem, trial or tribulation we face each day, day after day, as fallible human beings. Yet "Americans" seem all too willing to cede their freedom to an amorphous mass of unthinking government order-followers, whose one-size-fits-all approach to life is violence and a cage.

We have become a nation of misanthropic cry babies with 911 on speed-dial. Stop it, America. Enough is enough.

Huntsville, Alabama Police Department

American law enforcement is undergoing a complete moral collapse, unable or unwilling to discern even the most basic tenets of humanity and decency. This is what happens when highly-disturbed individuals are hired as police officers and given free rein to do whatever they want, to whomever they want, without fear of reprisal.

Had there been such a fear of reprisal, a preacher would not have been arrested for disorderly conduct for preaching the Gospel of Jesus Christ from a public sidewalk - using only his non-amplified voice.

Is arresting a preacher for preaching the Gospel from a public sidewalk - using only his non-amplified voice - the reason you became a police officer, Officer Hurt? Or did you choose not to disclose that information to the collection of highly-disturbed individuals who hired you as a police officer?

CHAPTER SIXTEEN

How to Kill the Constitution with Six Words

Freedom is measured by how willing we are to
submit to another person's authority.

Six words are all that stand between freedom and tyranny. With six words the United States of America is transformed into just another failed totalitarian police state. Six words and suddenly law *enforcers* become law *givers*, overtaking the Constitution as the supreme law of the land: "I'm giving you a lawful order!"

Six words and suddenly law *enforcers* become law *givers*, overtaking the Constitution as the supreme law of the land: "I'm giving you a lawful order!"

They speak and we must obey, without question or hesitation, lest one be shackled and caged for such wanton insubordination! Unlimited power bestowed not upon mere mortals, but upon those who fancy themselves as Gods.

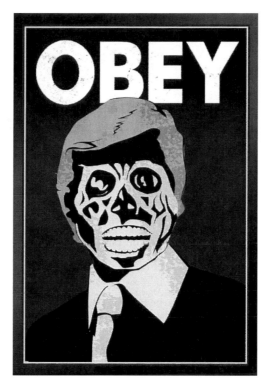

From Greer, South Carolina to Tucson, Arizona; from Worcester, Massachusetts to Leon Valley, Texas; oathbreakers are couching unspeakable tyranny behind so-called "lawful orders", with absolutely no regard for either their appropriateness or their legality. An order is not automatically lawful just because an oathbreaker says it is. That is not how the law works. Yet they keep doing it, with nothing to indicate that they intend to stop anytime soon.

Freedom is gone in these instances, crushed underfoot by a gang of totalitarian psychopaths too steeped in their sense of self-importance to understand the true nature of tyranny. It is nothing less than an illness, a bone-deep pathology, to actually believe that one human being has that kind of unfettered power over another human being. In essence, oathbreakers are America's "Supreme Law Lords", in the same manner as Herr Hitler.

North Little Rock, Arkansas Police Department

"Hey, man, in the future, just listen to the police. You have to listen to everything the police tell you!" Patrol Officer Jon Crowder scolded a suspect. It was the second time Crowder had lectured the suspect to obey everything a police officer said.

Along with so many of his cohorts, Crowder held the malignant belief that he could lawfully compel behavior (under the threat of arrest) simply by opening his mouth. Speak and the constitutional rights of every American vanish from the face of the earth. Who in the chain of command led them to believe that this was always and forever a legally acceptable enforcement tool, to wield over free people like Thor's Hammer?

At the time he was being admonished by Crowder, the suspect was sitting handcuffed in the back of a police car enduring unimaginable pain. Understandable, since Crowder had dislocated both of the man's shoulders and broken both of the man's arms during the arrest. What is so uniquely appalling about Crowder's appeal to blind obedience was the sick and twisted way Crowder used the very notion of a lawful order as a smokescreen to hide his criminal behavior.

Crowder had issued no "lawful order", the kind of order a reasonable person would conclude is relevant and acceptable under the circumstances, but which the man subsequently disobeyed. Crowder was trying to convince the backup officers, and whoever would review the dashboard video later on, that his abusive behavior was somehow justified because the man had not *listened* to what he was being told, not because the man had *resisted* what he was being told.

Lying was the only thing Crowder could use in his defense. Think of it as a teacher trying to convince other teachers that a totally cooperative and attentive student - who was suspected of chewing gum in class - deserved to have both arms broken for not spitting out the gum, even though he was never told to spit out the gum. It was the MERE EXISTENCE of obedience to an authority figure that Crowder was appealing to.

Because the man MAY have disobeyed Crowder, had Crowder CHOSEN to issue a lawful order, he got what he deserved. Crowder brutalized the man for something Crowder never said, for actions the man never took. It was done because an "officer of the law" had been granted "special powers" by the ruling class, who used those special powers to physically harm another human being. Then, after the deed was done, Crowder told his fellow officers it was a necessary use of force because instant obedience to police authority was presumed.

What Little Rock Police Officer Jon Crowder did that day would eventually lead to his arrest for 3rd-degree battery (a simple misdemeanor) and a $30,000 settlement for the man whose arms he had broken - the arms Crowder broke AFTER the man was handcuffed.

Effingham County, Georgia Sheriff's Department
In July 2019, an Effingham County Sheriff's Deputy stopped to check on the welfare of a man who had parked his car on the shoulder of a local highway to use his cell phone. "I'm fine. I'm thumbs up. I'm good!" the driver told the deputy.

She insisted on seeing the man's driver's license (i.e. his free-dom papers). "Just give me your driver's license so I can run you and make sure you're good," the deputy said.

Regardless, her request to see the man's driver's license was well within the deputy's lawful authority. Police officers are allowed to ask questions. In this case, the deputy refused to accept "no" for an answer. When two more deputies arrived as backup, both the Constitution and the man's Fourth Amendment right against unrea-sonable searches and seizures were about to get flushed.

Without so much as reasonable suspicion of a crime, one of the backup deputies first asked, then demanded, that the man get out of the car. When the driver balked, the second backup deputy screamed, "GET THE [EXPLETIVE] OUT OF THE CAR! YOU'RE ABOUT TO GET TASED!"

This same deputy unlocked the car door and, working as a team, the deputies were able to remove the driver from the car. He was ultimately charged with "obstructing an official investigation", supposedly for not providing his driver's license in a timely manner and because he failed to answer questions after his arrest. Who knew the U.S. Supreme Court had carved out Fourth and Fifth Amendment exceptions for the Effingham County Sheriff's Department?

The first disturbing takeaway is how deputies had used "lawful orders" to compel the behavior of an innocent man. As if to prove my point, one of the deputies said during the arrest, "When a deputy tells you to do something, YOU DO IT!" Just like that. The second takeaway is the violent nature of the deputy's threat to use a Taser, mixed with a healthy dose of profanity.

As for the sheriff's deputy who said she had stopped to check on the man's welfare, I would hope the uniform pants she was wearing that day were made of fire-retardant Nomex.

Austin, Texas Police Department

An activist filming a nighttime traffic stop was approached by two backup patrol officers: James Maufrais, with the heavily-tattooed forearms, and his trusty sidekick, Jesse Lane. Both officers shined their high-intensity flashlights straight into the man's camera lens, a violation of the Austin Police Department's written policy, which expressly prohibited officers from doing what Maufrais and Lane were doing to the activist.

Officer Maufrais verbally and physically threatened the activist to such an extent that he was barely able to restrain himself. He and Lane forced the activist to back up and up and up until the scene of the traffic stop was no longer visible in the distance. They kept forcing the activist to back up until they reached a crosswalk. "I'm giving you a lawful order to stay in the crosswalk!" Maufrais snarled. "You step one foot out of that crosswalk and I'm going to arrest you for failing to obey a lawful order!"

Maufrais was borderline psychotic. By his actions that night, Maufrais had made clear his deep-seated hatred for humanity, the rule of law, and the Constitution. As an oathbreaker, what mattered to Maufrais was serving whatever was in his best interest.

Even more disgusting is when it was learned that Maufrais had only recently returned from a deployment in Afghanistan. With that fact alone, Maufrais had disgraced not one but two uniforms. He had violated not one but two oaths. How dare you, Officer Maufrais.

Austin Chief of Police Art Acevedo later suspended Maufrais for twenty days without pay and Lane for ten days without pay. "Self-inflicted stupidity" is how Chief Acevedo described the officers' conduct that night. No kidding, Chief.

Prichard, Alabama Police Department

Known for its quaint southern hospitality, the town of Prichard, like the sleepy little hamlet of Pevely, Missouri, has a reputation for hiring some truly outstanding police officers. More felony arrests have been made in Prichard than in almost any other small town in Alabama; that is, if Prichard police officers are counted among the total.

"You need to stop filming! It's against the law in Alabama to film the police!" a Prichard Police Captain yelled at two activists as they were filming their encounter with the Captain outside the Prichard Police Department. "The Supreme Court says you have to obey an officer!"

Whether the Captain's statement is true or not is a moot point if the Captain believes it to be true, along with the other 899,999 officers who may believe it to be true. Therein lies the true imperilment to freedom.

Los Angeles County, California Sheriff's Department

A woman was filming a nighttime traffic stop from a public sidewalk when she was aggressively approached by Sheriff's Deputy Ortiz and ordered to move back. It was either move back or risk being arrested for "obstructing (the deputy's) investigation", even though the woman was already an acceptable distance away when Ortiz ordered her to move.

Albeit reluctantly, the woman moved back to the exact spot on the sidewalk the deputy had indicated - yet she was battered and arrested nonetheless. Onlookers recounted that it took the spineless tyrant 25 steps to get to where the woman was now standing to make the arrest.

As she was being led away in handcuffs, the woman pleaded with the deputies that she had done nothing wrong. It turned out that the woman was on a mission to hold police officers to a higher level of accountability after her son had been shot and killed by police the previous year.

New Jersey State Police

On the night of October 16, 2015, just outside of Philadelphia, New Jersey State Police Troopers Matthew Stazzone and Demetric Gosa arrested a female driver for "criminal obstruction" when she chose to remain silent during a routine traffic stop. Despite providing all requested documents, the woman was given a "lawful order" to answer the trooper's question "Do you know why you're being pulled over tonight?"

It was a probative question intended to get the woman to inadvertently incriminate herself by confirming the reason she had been stopped. She was under no legal obligation to answer the trooper's question. Likewise, the trooper had no business trying to force the woman to answer a question the trooper should have asked and answered himself.

Forced from the car, the woman was handcuffed and escorted to a waiting patrol car, where she was read her Miranda Warnings; a legal reminder that she had the right to remain silent and request the presence of an attorney prior to being questioned.

The woman was never formally charged with a crime; and the Police State of New Jersey kindly offered to pay the towing bill. How gentlemanly of them! The fact that she had been arrested for remaining silent *before* the arrest, then told she had the right to remain silent *after* the arrest, is jaw-dropping incompetence.

Well played, guys. By the way, did I happen to mention the woman was an attorney?

Lenawee County, Michigan Sheriff's Department

"If you're asked to do something, it's a lawful order!" Just like that.

CHAPTER SEVENTEEN

Freedom Papers

Checking for warrants is an unhealthy obsession among police officers, to the point where the Constitution no longer exists.

In 1852, Joseph Trammell registered as a free person in Loudon, Virginia and continued to do so every two years until 1865. During slavery, legally free blacks were required to register with county courts and secure "Certificates of Freedom", also known as freedom papers. For Trammell and other free blacks, carrying their papers was necessary to avoid being mistaken as a fugitive and enslaved.

Nowadays, freedom papers are called either a "driver's license" or "identification card". Free human beings who have committed no crime, yet fail to provide either document upon demand of a law enforcement officer, will be placed in chains and thrown into a cage until they surrender their identity.* This travesty has been brought to light in many of the previous accounts.

There are two settings where an oathbreaker will almost certainly try to hem someone up over their ID: a call for service (with no reported crime) and during a traffic stop. What invariably gets the ball rolling on the former is when a concerned citizen calls 911 to report "suspicious activity".

Although the caller failed to specify a crime, the matter has already escalated by virtue of the call being placed to 911; the number set aside for reporting emergencies. It escalates again when 911 passes along the report to a patrol officer, who then escalates the situation further if he rolls up to the scene determined to make an arrest.

*Under √ **Brown v. Texas (1979) and Hiibel v. Sixth Judicial Circuit Court (2004),** it was clarified by the U.S. Supreme Court that police officers CANNOT demand identification without first articulating reasonable suspicion of a particular crime.

ID CARD

BUSINESS
NAME:
ADDRESS:
PHONE:

BICYCLIST
NAME:
3-DIGIT ID #:

*Carry this ID card at all times.

This is a summary of what typically transpires, laid out in linear fashion: citizen calls 911 to report no crime > 911 passes along the report of no crime to the patrol officer > patrol officer arrives to investigate the report of no crime > the report of no crime is used as the reason to detain and demand ID > person refuses to surrender ID on constitutional grounds, having not committed a crime > patrol officer arrests the person for failing to ID and/or obstructing a non-criminal investigation > innocent person is placed in chains and thrown into a cage for not committing a crime > patrol officer is hired as the next Chief of Police for Leon Valley, Texas.

Oathbreakers in these circumstances investigate nothing; unlawfully detain over nothing; auger down for ID over nothing; falsely arrest over nothing; and ruin a life because they want to. This unconstitutional behavior by oathbreakers is so common, one would think they attended the same police academy and were trained by the same foggy-headed instructor.

Without question, it is the latter setting of a routine traffic stop where an oathbreaker is most likely to try to hem someone up over their ID; specifically, an innocent passenger. There is something about a traffic stop that makes officers believe the car's occupants have forfeited their constitutional rights the moment they stepped into the car (most notably, the totalitarian mutants with the Los Angeles County Sheriff's Department).

As a reminder, innocent passengers do not have to surrender their ID to law enforcement. However, the passengers are considered to be legally detained during a lawful traffic stop and must step out of the car when told to do so.

Demanding an innocent person surrender their identification continues to be the primary "portal" through which oathbreakers enter to try to deprive a citizen of their constitutional rights. Either surrender your freedom papers or go to jail.

Colorado Springs, Colorado Police Department

Undergoing a lobotomy must be a prerequisite to becoming a Colorado Springs police officer. Consider what happened to a parent who had parked his car near a local middle school, waiting to pick up his son after a school event. He was contacted unexpectedly by several of Colorado Springs' finest, who said they were investigating a report of a "suspicious vehicle".

Whether the claim was true is irrelevant. What is true is the way the officers were going to milk the "suspicious vehicle/person" claim for everything they could. Worth mentioning about this incident is how it exposed many of the parlor tricks that oathbreakers use to make unconstitutional detentions or arrests. It is therefore worthy of dissection.

Pay close attention to how the officers zero in on trying to get the man to surrender his ID. Above all else is to remember that mere suspicion is not reasonable suspicion, which is the minimum standard to lawfully detain under a Terry Stop. A person lawfully detained under a Terry Stop is required to identify themselves to police.

At the time of contact, the man was legally parked and the headlights were on. Criminals do not usually park their car at night with the headlights on. Nor in the midst of potential witnesses. Not that it mattered to a gaggle of incompetent Colorado Springs police officers. Which raises the question of whether or not it is redundant to use "Colorado Springs police officer" and "incompetent" in the same sentence?

What follows is a partial transcript of the officers' remarks to the man in "quotations"; followed by my best attempt to explain their rationale:

1. "Step out of the vehicle and we'll talk." - Officer(s) wanted the man out of the car, probably to perform an unlawful and unconstitutional pat-down for weapons (author: what I find especially troubling about an officer's lawful ability to order [innocent] passenger(s) to step from the vehicle, is that its strictest intent was to foster officer safety by allowing officers to control subject placement during traffic stops. Instead, oathbreakers see it as an opportunity to conduct random pat-downs for weapons, without reasonable suspicion that the passenger had committed a crime, or that the passenger may be armed and/or overtly dangerous). During the exchange, an officer made reference to Pennsylvania v. Mimms. Of course they would twist case law. Why not, if it can be used as a means to an end? A legal decision that facilitated officer safety - by allowing officers to control subject placement during a

lawful traffic stop - was being used to facilitate a malicious motive. Give incompetent cops with malicious motives an inch, they will take as much as they can get away with. This is especially true during traffic stops, where oathbreakers pretty much do whatever they want with no regard for the Constitution.

2. "You do have to step out. We can get this done real quick." - The officer was implying that the eventual outcome would be determined by the man's level of cooperation, unrelated to whether or not he had actually committed a crime. This common parlor trick is called an "appeal to appeasement". If the man were to just give up his rights, he would be let go. An "appeal to appeasement" is an especially disconcerting parlor trick because an oathbreaker can use it to coerce all sorts of rights-robbing behavior.

3. "We're investigating suspicious circumstances." - What "suspicious circumstances"? Procedurally speaking, police do not investigate "suspicious circumstances". They investigate CRIMES. What should be clear by now is how oathbreakers will use so-called "suspicious circumstances" to segue into unconstitutional detentions. Moreover, officers who insist on treating "suspicious circumstances" on par with a suspected crime are prone to manufacture probable cause to arrest.

4. "Do you have an ID on you? Can I get your ID? I'm asking you to step out of the vehicle." - In some police jurisdictions, the man would have been dragged from the car and arrested; charged with some manufactured crime like "obstructing an investigation". What I am

witnessing over and over in these encounters is how oathbreakers will use a charge of criminal obstruction as a way to punish an innocent person for not cooperating. Taken to its most extreme level, what would prevent an officer from using a charge of obstructing an investigation as a means to punish someone for not confessing to a crime? Does failing to confess, on its face, not obstruct or impede an investigation? Given their predilection to use a charge of obstructing an investigation as a catch-all charge, it makes me wonder if this is a manifestation of poor training? Or is it a byproduct of watching their counterparts getting away with it time after time on YouTube?

5. "I'm holding onto you, sir. Step out of the vehicle. I got you, and we'll get you along. I need you to step out of the vehicle." - Still no articulation of a crime. Another implied promise to end the contact, if only the man were to identify himself. The man had already explained numerous times that he was waiting to pick up his son. This should have ended the contact the first time it was asked and answered.

6. "Just cooperate. Cooperate, okay?" - First, they tried intimidation to get his ID and failed. This particular officer was almost pleading with the man. By this point, the officers knew full-well they had pushed a bad position. Frustration over the man's stubbornness was giving way to panic. They had made themselves look like fools. Pride was coming to the fore.

7. "The reason we're contacting you specifically and asking for your ID...is that you're sitting over here all

by yourself. It's strange with everything else going on. We're asking you for your identification and we'll be on our way." - Being by himself was deemed "strange"? Believing someone is strange as the sole reason to detain had just joined its kissing cousin, "I'm investigating suspicious activity", alongside the rest of the "I have no idea what I'm doing" trophies sitting atop the mantle of the oathbreaker fireplace.

8. "We don't know you, sir." - This is what an officer said immediately after the man once again denied doing anything illegal. Of course they did not know the man. So what? It is not as if they are on a first-name basis with everyone they contact. Oathbreakers who desire to do bad things seem to believe that unfamiliarity is just cause to ignore the Constitution.

9. "Because you're not identifying yourself, sir." - They had walked up to an innocent man and demanded his ID, then said he was being detained for not surrendering his ID! Outrageous! This maneuver is torn straight from the Nazi playbook. Moreover, it portends the collapse of law and order by shredding the presumption of innocence. Police must never be allowed to demand identification from an innocent person. Never!

10. "If you didn't want this to turn into a whole ordeal, all you had to do was identify yourself." - This is called "flipping the script" where the officers had purposefully shifted the legal burden from themselves to the man. Whatever the problem, it was the man's fault for not cooperating. It was, in fact, the unprofessional and

unconstitutional conduct of the officers that created the "whole ordeal" in the first place.

11. "How are we supposed to know who you are if you're not identifying yourself?" - This is called "circular reasoning". The officers demanded ID because they did not know the man. Because they did not know the man, the officers demanded ID. It was none of their business who the man was without first establishing reasonable suspicion of a particular crime. The officers were no longer trying to flip the script at this point; they were trying to deny the man his Fourth Amendment right to privacy as a whole. If the man were indeed breaking one or more laws, why had he not already been arrested?

12. "I'm the training officer." - This admission was made shortly after the man asked the officers to disclose their official job titles. It explained a lot of what was going on. An incompetent training officer was training baby cops to become incompetent cops. What were the odds the training officer was the instigator?

San Bernardino County, California Sheriff's Department

During a minor traffic stop, Deputy Quezada went straight for the front seat passenger's ID.* In an interaction that was almost painful to watch, a clueless Quezada invoked the same unconstitutional claptrap as his peers when he demanded that the passenger surrender her freedom papers. Here are some gems from oathbreaker Quezada:

1. "Everybody inside a vehicle during a traffic stop needs to be identified and provide their driver's license. You understand that, right?"

2. "Step out of the vehicle, ma'am. I'm going to pat you down, make sure you don't have any weapons. Ma'am, can I see your ID (makes the international symbol for requesting ID)?"

3. "You do understand that you need to provide identification? I'm going to place you in handcuffs and place you in the back of my vehicle! You do understand that you're not going to win this?"

> **"You do understand that you're not going to win this?"**

4. "Everybody inside the vehicle during a traffic stop is going to be detained, will be detained, and everybody will be ID'd. So, here's your last chance, before I place you in handcuffs. This is your last chance before I place you in handcuffs, okay?"

5. "You're being detained and you're going to be placed in handcuffs, okay? I have the right to ID you! You have to be identified when you're being detained, okay? If you give it to me, I'll take you out of handcuffs!" (author: precisely how long was Deputy Quezada willing to detain the handcuffed woman as he waited for her to surrender her personal information? It is incomprehensible to think that something like this can occur in the United States of America).

6. "How do I know you're not a parolee at large or someone that has a felony warrant? I don't know who you are!"

*While Deputy Quezada's lack of knowledge about the law may seem amusing, never forget how quickly the situation could have turned violent.

Kingsland, Georgia Police Department

Recently, a 17-year-old man was filming near his home when he was confronted by Kingsland Patrol Officers Brandon Todd and Samantha Swartz. A concerned citizen had called 911 to report that a "suspicious person" was taking pictures of homes, with no mention of criminal activity. Not that it would have mattered. After 9/11, concerns replaced crimes as reasonable suspicion to detain and probable cause to arrest.

Star-crossed pendejos

Proving once again that oathbreakers are a one-trick pony, the officers demanded to see the young man's ID, with Todd saying crudely "You're beginning to [expletive] me off!" when the young man failed to comply. "We have the right to ID you!" the officers said almost in unison. "Someone called 911 and reported suspicious activity!"

WRONG! There was only ONE WAY they could make such a claim, which was there had to be a law requiring the subject of a 911 call to identify themselves.

Now on foot, the oathbreakers followed the young man down the street for half a block before he was placed under arrest for failing to surrender ID. Had the pair of star-crossed pendejos even one brain between them, they only had to follow the young man to his house a few blocks away and speak with a parent to confirm his identity.

In what was a final display of utter disrespect before heading to jail, Officer Todd taunted the young man by calling his father a "Sovereign Citizen". "Sovereign Citizen" is an intentionally disparaging, us vs. them term used frequently by oathbreakers to describe a person who asserts their constitutional rights during police interactions. In truth, it is law enforcement who are the real Sovereign Citizens by virtue of their being shielded from most claims of misconduct by Qualified Immunity.

Rhode Island State Police

A car's front-seat passenger - a naturalized U.S. citizen from Cuba and most likely profiled - unexpectedly found himself staring at the gun belts of five Rhode Island state troopers, who collectively badgered the man to surrender his ID. They wanted to check the man for warrants, of course, only with a twist.

If there were a warrant and the man was arrested, the troopers would have undoubtedly searched the car. A search could lead to the discovery of illegal contraband, which is the reason there were five state troopers stacked just outside the passenger door. They were performing highway drug interdiction and their motives were anything but pure.

Law enforcement agencies receive federal funding to implement drug interdiction programs at the state and local levels. It is a lucrative business, so to keep the money rolling in agencies have to show results. Tossed into the mix is something called "federal overtime", which puts extra cash in an officer's pocket. This means officers are now monetarily incentivized to trample on the rights of innocent drivers and passengers.

In furtherance of the goals of drug interdiction and putting some extra cash in their pockets, one trooper had the gall to tell the man that he lost his constitutional rights inside of a car. Step inside the car and lose one's rights, step outside of the car and those rights are magically restored - a difference of maybe three feet? That is exactly what the trooper had just said.

Following in the wake of Trooper Comrade Commissar's stunningly stupid statement, a second trooper said something similarly stupid when he told the man that he could stop a bus driver for speeding and order the passengers to surrender their identification. What an outrageous claim to make, to suggest that an innocent passenger on a bus could go to jail for refusing to surrender their ID? When did the Rhode Island State Police adopt the "North Korean Model of Community Policing"? These troopers were either delusional, lying, or both.

Under the threat of arrest, the foreign-born passenger eventually surrendered his ID (no aspersions intended, since he probably knew his rights better than most). Never in my life would I have thought that two law enforcement officers could stoop so low, to callously intimidate a citizen into surrendering his ID as a means to an end. This is why citizens must 1) know their rights, 2) film their interactions with the police, and 3) never assume that a police officer is their friend.

Little Elm, Texas Police Department
It was a disturbance call at a private residence with no known victim of a crime, other than the male resident of the home had called the police to help remove a troublesome woman from the premises. Albeit reluctantly, the man allowed the officers to enter the residence (big mistake) even after the situation with the woman had been largely resolved.

In a few short minutes, the contact went from needing the man's personal information for a supposed "log entry", to being detained under the threat of arrest unless he surrendered his ID.

"Why do I have to give you my ID?" the man quizzed the officer. "I didn't commit a crime!" "But I don't know that!" the instigator answered, which was an inadvertent admission that the officer was on a fishing expedition. Moreover, it was a lost opportunity to take control of the narrative by flipping the script. Without knowing a crime had occurred, why was the officer demanding the resident's ID?

When the resident again refused, he was placed in chains and thrown into a cage for the dystopian-like crime of "defiance of authority" for failing to surrender his freedom papers. Officers had created probable cause to arrest where none had previously existed, because checking for warrants overrides the Constitution in the mind of an oathbreaker. **NOTE:** As is the case with countless other agencies, there is obviously something very wrong with the Little Elm Police Department. Only recently, three patrol officers beat an activist into the ground after an officer on a traffic stop ordered him to move back. The activist was a safe distance from the stop and was in no way interfering with the officer. This has become a regular occurrence with police: ordering activists to move back some arbitrary distance under the threat of arrest. Legality notwithstanding, it has become widespread for the simple reason that it works.

Hibbing, Minnesota Police Department

Some officers refuse to get it. Take Sergeant Brent Everett, for example. It took Sergeant Everett and a companion officer just under four minutes to grossly violate the civil rights of an activist, who had purportedly taken pictures near the local Armory. What happened that day in Hibbing is a textbook case of an officer rushing in to make an arrest and making himself look like a fool.

Angry and confrontational, Sergeant Everett unlawfully detained the activist; demanded ID; needlessly escalated the situation by telling the backup officer that the activist was being "non-compliant" (a coward's move); and threatened to arrest the activist for not following his commands. Everett continually looked over his right shoulder waiting for the backup officer to arrive, which is what oathbreakers like Everett do when they run out of options.

"Put your hands behind your back! You're under arrest!" screeched an out of control Sergeant Everett just seconds before he and the freshly-arrived backup officer face-planted the activist into the ground. Everett then seized both of the activist's cameras, cut off his backpack, and searched him and his property without so much as reasonable suspicion of a crime. Mighty fine police work there, Sarge!

Sergeant Everett charged the activist with the catch-all charge of "obstructing an officer" for failing to provide his identification, which had nothing to do with obstructing anything (Sgt. Everett had manufactured probable cause to arrest when, in fact, none had existed UNTIL EVERETT SHOWED UP). Adding insult to injury was the fact that the activist was made to wait five months before the Hibbing Police Department returned the items that Everett stole when he kidnapped the activist.

In his Findings of Fact, St. Louis County District Court Judge Mark M. Starr concluded that, although Sergeant Everett had "acted reasonably and with good intentions" (huh?), he had failed to articulate reasonable suspicion of a crime and the charge was dismissed. Then came the Findings' last sentence, in which Judge Starr implied it was the activist's fault for the incident. Starr wrote, "Had (Mr. Swanson) cooperated with law enforcement and explained to them what he was doing, the situation probably would have ended without issue."

No, Judge Starr, it was not up to the activist to convince Sergeant Everett of anything. Rather, it was up to Sergeant Everett to know the law.

Nowhere am I suggesting that officers are obliged to stand patiently and listen carefully to every word a person has to say. What I am suggesting is that officers use the totality of the circumstances to guide their decisions, rather than making a rush to judgment. Never in the history of humankind has anyone ever made a good decision when its foundation was built upon raw human emotion. This applies equally to both police officers and citizens.

Why do oathbreakers like Sergeant Everett do what they do? Because they lack basic humanity. Because they lack character. Because they are self-absorbed narcissists who demand instant obedience and unearned respect. Because they have some other undisclosed personality defect. Because they know they will get away with it.

Because they are ignorant of the law. Because they are poor listeners. Because they allow their egos to override their ability to make sound decisions. Because the only arrow in their law enforcement quiver is ARREST! Because they view the Constitution as meaningless, if it even exists at all.

Walker, Louisiana Police Department

Officer Silve is arrogant, unprofessional, and one more member of the "Clueless Cop Club". Silve rolled up on an activist and almost immediately demanded the activist surrender her ID. She politely declined, taking time to remind Officer Silve that she only had to provide ID if she were suspected of a crime. Click! "Y'all required to show ID, bein' y'all suspicious," Silve said with a distinct Louisiana drawl.

Soon more officers arrived on the scene, including Police Chief David Addison. "She ain't doin' nothin' wrong. She out here filming, which is no problem," Silve dutifully reported to the Chief, "but what she doin' is suspicious. In the State of Louisiana, y'all gotta give up your ID to a police officer!"

Chief Addison nodded his head in agreement. "In the State of Louisiana, when an officer asks y'all a question, y'all gotta answer. Otherwise, it's called resisting arrest!" the Chief of the Clueless Cop

Club said erroneously. A plain-clothes detective chirped, "Y'all gotta show ID, otherwise it's called resisting an officer!"

Cajun-style accents aside, this level of incompetence in law enforcement is as chilling as it is rampant. Three male officers were intending to use violence against a young woman, who had not committed a crime, because not one of the officers knew the law or what they were doing. As a result, they defaulted into ARREST! mode and came dangerously close to ruining her life.

Under the duress of being threatened with arrest, the activist eventually surrendered her information. Who would want to end up in a jail cell in the most corrupt, good ol' boy state in the nation, other than its neighboring state to the east, Mississippi?

The activist has since met with a civil rights attorney. Folklore has it that on the day of her illegal detention - when Chief Addison nodded his head in approval - the sound of rocks bouncing around the inside of a tin can could be heard all the way to Moscow.

Cranston, Rhode Island Police Department

On September 2, 2018, Officer Andrea P. Comella responded to a call involving a "suspicious person" believed to be filming the headquarters building of the Rhode Island National Guard. Comella proved to be just another incompetent oathbreaker determined to take a massive dump on the Constitution.

Officer Comella displayed not a modicum of professionalism during her interaction with the activist. Like every other incompetent oathbreaker, Comella demanded the activist surrender his ID under the claim that his behavior was suspicious. Sound familiar? When the activist refused to give up his ID, Comella said, "Well, until I can determine that you are NOT committing a crime, I'm going to ask you for your ID."

How ridiculous, as though getting hold of the activist's ID would have somehow helped determine if a crime was being committed. As a police officer, Comella's job is not to determine whether a crime is NOT being committed. If that were true, we would all end up in jail for the crimes we did not commit!

Too late. A mostly out of control Comella went hands-on as soon as she had assembled a gang of her fellow Cranston police officers. It was chains and a cage for the activist, having been arrested for obstruction of justice and disorderly conduct. For Comella, professionalism and requisite objectivity were as foreign a concept as the Constitution and Bill of Rights.

Limited thinking must be a job requirement for the Cranston Police Department. If filming a National Guard facility was suspicious enough to warrant a free trip to jail, what would Comella have done had she looked across the street and spotted a hipster filming the facility simultaneously from his well-manicured front lawn?

What about the person seen filming the headquarters from across the street, while peering out the hipster's bedroom window? Or the person who takes a picture of the M-60 Main Battle Tank the National Guard has displayed on the front lawn? Or the person peering through a telephoto lens from a mile away?

If the issue is strictly filming, then why should it matter how near or how far the person is standing in relation to the facility, or the reason for filming in the first place?

Colonel Michael Winquist, Cranston Chief of Police, said he supported Comella's "excellent" handling of the incident, noting her efforts to de-escalate the situation. De-escalate the situation? Was Winquist high on his own supply at the time? Or did his words of support have anything to do with Comella's father having once served as the Cranston Chief of Police?

LaPorte, Texas Police Department

An incident between an activist and members of the LaPorte Police Department (k9 officer Barry Groaning and Patrol Sergeant Ayers) culminated in the arrest of the activist for failure to ID after the activist was seen filming the police station where the officers worked.

Everything focused on getting hold of the activist's ID. Here, in their own words, is the proof:

1. "Are you authorized to be here? No, you're not being detained. Do you have ID? You're being detained for suspicious circumstances. Let me see your ID! Can I ask why you're filming our building?"

2. "It's a government facility. You're causing alarm and people are calling in on you. Did you get permission from dispatch? Do you have ID on you? You're not answering my questions!"

3. "Do you have any ID on you? We would like to know who you are, for the very simple reason that terrorist acts do occur! If you're going to record anything, you have to get permission!"

4. "Are you going to give me identification or not? You will be (arrested) if you don't hand me identification right now, so I can identify who you are! What I'm trying to do is take care of a suspicious person [not breaking the law], at a suspicious place [a public sidewalk], at a suspicious time [broad daylight]."

5. "Put him in jail!"

As the activist was being herded into the jail, Sgt. Ayers admitted there were no charges that could be filed. Yet the activist was forced to go through the booking process and sit in a cage for two hours before being released. They got the job done by going after his freedom papers, because protecting and serving their best interest is what oathbreakers do best.

West Des Moines, Iowa Police Department, and the Polk County Prosecutor's Office

"The Mournful Tale of the Rock and the Post", starring West Des Moines Police Officer Clinton "the Rock" Ray & Polk County Prosecutor Thomas "the Post" Tolbert.*

One afternoon, a good-natured fellow by the name of Emmett Cooper-Hansen was driving down a dusty trail in the middle of Iowa farm country, when he happened to catch a glimpse of a flat rock resting atop an old wooden fence post. Emmett Cooper-Hansen pulled to the side of the road to check it out.

"Mister! Hey Mister!" the rock and the post cried out in unison. "Any chance you'd be headed down to West Des Moines, Iowa? We could surely use a ride, seeing as we ain't got no legs!" Lo and behold, that's where Emmett Cooper-Hansen was headed! "Sure t'ing 'dere, fellas! Be happy to oblige!"

Emmett Cooper-Hansen helped the rock and the post pack a few belongings and carried them to the car. Off they went, with the rock and the post settled comfortably in the back seat. Reinvigorated and full of optimism, the rock serenaded the post with "Papa was a Rollin' Stone" by The Temptations!

Soon enough, the trio pulled into West Des Moines, Iowa. "Where to, fellas?" Emmett Cooper-Hansen asked the rock and the post. "Take me to the police station!" the rock eagerly exclaimed. "Take me to the prosecutor's office!" the post peeled. "We have job interviews!"

So Emmett Cooper-Hansen dropped the rock at the station and the post at the office and spent the time waiting at the nearby Greasy Spoon Cafe. "Sure hope 'dat t'ings work out for da boys," Emmett Cooper-Hansen said between sips of tepid coffee. "Dem boys really want dem 'dere jobs!"

Exactly one hour later, Emmett Cooper-Hansen drove to the station to pick up the rock and to the office to pick up the post. The boys were devastated! Morose, even! "You boys look all done in. What happened over 'dere?" Emmett Cooper-Hansen asked the mournful pair.

The rock looked at the post, the post looked at the rock. With one voice they cried, "They told us we were over-qualified!"

*West Des Moines Police Officer Clinton "the Rock" Ray responded to a report of a man seen going door to door in a quiet, West Des Moines neighborhood. A bumbling Ray told the young man that he was being detained because he was a suspicious person, people in the neighborhood were concerned, and because he was not "doing what he was told". Ray went on to arrest the man for failing to surrender his freedom papers. Polk County Prosecutor Thomas "the Post" Tolbert then amended the charge to "harassing a public official" because the man had allegedly used profanity during his unconstitutional detention and false arrest. Sergeant Dan Wade, representing the thin blue line, said in a post-arrest interview with KCCI News, "It was absolutely above-board...the officer interacted in a way that we would expect him to." Sergeant Wade further counseled viewers to essentially obey everything an officer says. In other words, surrender your rights to incompetent oathbreakers like Ray and Tolbert. What had the "suspicious" man been doing prior to Officer Ray showing up and trying to ruin his life? As he tried to explain to the quivering Ray, he was canvassing voters prior to an upcoming election. It made no difference. An innocent man was caged by Officer Ray, besmirched by Sergeant Wade, and persecuted by prosecutor Tolbert for the heinous crime of encouraging his fellow citizens to vote. Outstanding!

Did I happen to mention the young man was black? Who said Jim Crow was dead?

Greer, South Carolina Police Department

Doing what is legal and constitutional means nothing to an oathbreaker like Lieutenant J. Holcombe of the Greer Police Department. He is just one of the countless police officers who will gladly put their best interest ahead of freedom; who will manufacture a crime, when necessary, to shut down a constitutionally protected activity such as public photography.

Emboldened by the presence of his fellow uniformed gang members, the stuttering and red-faced Lieutenant Holcombe never even tried to be objective. He went after the activist's ID, at one point tossing out the Constitution-killing phrase "in this day and age" as an excuse to demand ID. It is a coward's phrase, one used by trembling oathbreakers afraid of the camera-toting boogie man. (For Holcombe's benefit, the origin of "in this day and age" can be traced all the way back to when Cain slew Abel. Things have been going downhill ever since.)

Lt. Holcombe, keeping the southern tradition alive.

Arresting the activist for filming the police station, along with filming the police station's top-secret parking lot, was a foregone conclusion. He was swarmed, handcuffed, and falsely arrested for "interfering with a police officer", which is just another way of saying "obstructing an investigation". Holcombe would not shut his mouth during the arrest, telling the activist glibly, "Guess what? You're about to see the inside of a South Carolina jail!"

Of course the Greer city attorney supported the actions of the officers, claiming in a news release that it was the fault of the activist for acting suspiciously and failing to identify himself. Typical government obfuscation, shifting the blame to avoid a lawsuit and taint any future jury pool. It sickens me the way that government workers treat buildings like people and people like buildings, as though buildings (and parking lots) have a reasonable expectation of privacy but human beings do not.

As is the case with Virginia, South Carolina is one of the "Antebellum" states of the old South (c. 1800-1865) where free blacks were required to carry and display their freedom papers. Lieutenant Holcombe kept the southern tradition alive when he placed the African-American activist in chains for failing to surrender his freedom papers. Obviously, nothing has changed down in the "Palmetto State".

Cook County, Illinois Sheriff's Department

In March 2018, an activist was filming the front of the Cook County Courthouse in Bridgeview, Illinois. The activist's presence drew the attention of several Cook County Sheriff's Deputies, including an on-site supervisor with the last name of Milazzo.

Deputy Milazzo's self-inflicted incompetence was on full display the moment he made contact with the activist. Reaching deep into his bag of sarcastic voices, the intrepid Milazzo asked the activist, "Ma'am, you know this is a public building?" Uh oh, Milazzo was already well on his way to becoming the next YouTube Phenom.

When the activist asked what law prevented her from filming the building, Milazzo sputtered, "Judicial law!" as though judges make the laws, Deputy Milazzo. They only think they do. "You can't tape the building," Milazzo continued, "so we're going to go inside and we're going to ID you!"

Asked if she were being detained, a sputtering Milazzo answered, "Yes, you are being detained because you're doing something suspicious, and we're going to take you inside and we're going to ID you!" Deputy "Dum Dum" Milazzo turned to a second clueless deputy and said, "Who's got a set of 'cuffs? She doesn't want to go agreeably!"

Now handcuffed, the activist was being escorted into the building on her way to see a federal magistrate when Milazzo spoke the immortal line that would have been musiqaa to Osama bin Laden's ears: "You're aware of homeland security, right?"

The activist was eventually released from custody without being charged and without giving up her ID. A federal lawsuit was filed on her behalf but the final outcome is unknown at the time of writing.

Prince William County, Virginia Police Department

"You can't take pictures of a government building!" Patrol Officer G. Walsh (pictured lower-left corner) of the Prince William County Police Department stated angrily to an activist,* after the activist was seen taking photographs of county buildings and property from a public sidewalk. "You need to identify yourself or that's going to be a crime!"

Badged Cowards

Now detained under the threat of violence, the activist was soon surrounded by no less than six oathbreakers from the Prince William County PD. These jack-booted criminals - working at the behest of the government - saw a free human being doing something they did not like and were determined to stop. This despite the activity being legal, harmless, and protected by the Constitution.

It was eighteen minutes from the time the stuttering Patrol Coward G. Walsh first made contact before the activist was swarmed and arrested. During those eighteen long minutes, the oath-breaking cowards manufactured accusation after accusation, crime after crime, to force the activist to surrender his identification - eventually topping out at sixteen: suspicious activity; people were concerned; in this day and age; wars are going on in other countries; a terrorist planning an attack; taking pictures of government property; failing to ID; refusing to cooperate; having something to hide; having an outstanding warrant; wearing a face mask in public (a supposed felony); wearing a face mask for non-religious purposes; failing to remove his face mask (which the activist did); disorderly conduct; creating a disturbance; and obstruction of justice.

Yet, they would have all magically disappeared if only the activist had identified himself. If only the young man had surrendered his Fourth Amendment rights, he could have been on his way.

If only Rosa Parks had given up her seat on the bus to a white man, she could have been on her way. If only.

*Activists like this young man put themselves in jeopardy every time they venture out to hold the police accountable. It takes guts to do what they do and many have been assaulted, arrested, and/ or had their lives ruined by the thin blue line. How surreal that citizens have more to fear from the police than any other group in the country. In addition, activists' names are well-known to law enforcement and their personal information is freely shared between agencies. Over what? For public photography, which is a perfectly legal and constitutionally protected activity? It cannot and does not rise to the level of reasonable suspicion of a crime, to be used as justification for either detention and/or arrest. Indicative of a society in decline is to walk outside with a camera and be thrown inside a cage by the police. These officers are not heroes. Nor do they deserve our respect. It is not up to us to get along with them, it is up to them to get along with us. They can start by treating us as human beings, or is that too much to ask of these public servants?

So, speaking on my own behalf, I would like to thank each civil rights activist for their willingness to fight tyranny; and to thank those who came before them and those who will follow.

CHAPTER EIGHTEEN

Checkpoints

*Without rigid oversight, checkpoints can
resemble a free-fire zone in combat.*

Another method oathbreakers use to skirt the
Constitution is by setting up various checkpoints along public highways. I am not opposed to clearly-marked and properly-operated
checkpoints. As a game warden, I worked numerous roadside game
checks where we conducted inspections of game and fish. However,
an inspection can only go forward after it has been established the
traveler is in possession of game.

"Are you in possession of wildlife or wildlife parts?" is the
question that was typically posed to travelers. Even then it was the
traveler - not the officer - who controlled the scope of the inspection.
If the traveler said there was game inside a pink Coleman cooler,
we only inspected the contents of the pink Coleman cooler. Those
travelers not in possession of game were simply "waved through",

with no more hassle other than having to stop briefly to be queried. Never were they forced to answer the question or forced to submit to an inspection.

To expand the limited scope of an inspection into a full-blown search, an officer would need a valid search warrant, knowing consent to search from the traveler, or probable cause the traveler was in possession of illegal contraband discovered lawfully under the Plain View Doctrine.

Various court rulings have affirmed that even though roadside game checks are considered a momentary seizure of the person, game and fish inspections are not unreasonable and are therefore permissible. Here is why: there is a reduced expectation of privacy in a motor vehicle; motor vehicles are highly-mobile; ill-gotten game can be easily disposed of; and states have a compelling interest to protect its wildlife resources on behalf of both consumptive and non-consumptive users alike.

Again, roadside game checks have been deemed constitutional as long as they are conducted within all legal parameters established by the courts.

Oathbreakers couldn't care less about the Constitution or whatever legal parameters have been established by the courts. Especially when it comes to DUI (Driving Under the Influence) checkpoints. Instead, they will use a DUI checkpoint as cover to unlawfully compel behavior they could otherwise never lawfully compel anywhere outside of the checkpoint √ (**Delaware v. Prouse 1979**).

An example is a motorist who complies with every directive they are given: stops at the checkpoint and rolls down the window far enough to allow an officer to "sniff" for the odor of an alcoholic beverage. So why is the sober traveler still being detained at the checkpoint?

It usually occurs when an overzealous officer demands the person surrender his or her driver's license; or submit to a field sobriety test, just because. This clearly exceeds the scope of most DUI checkpoints and is done without the benefit of the officer having to articulate reasonable suspicion of a crime. It is far more common than one might think.

Los Angeles, California Police Department

Pick any DUI checkpoint manned by the fine men and women of the LAPD. It is pretty much game over for the motorist who correctly asserts their constitutional rights. Police Lieutenant Michelle Loomis of the LAPD's Greater Los Angeles Area would know what I am talking about.

I would urge those interested to go to YouTube and carefully study Lieutenant Loomis' unprofessional conduct at a DUI checkpoint back in 2014, where Loomis and her LAPD cohorts forced a sober driver from his car. Pay special attention to Loomis as she belittles the driver using her trademark flat and lifeless tone of voice. She is without compassion. A tyrant who wears her "I don't give a [expletive] about the Constitution" demeanor like a badge of honor.

California Highway Patrol (CHP) and Hawthorne, California Police Department

On the night of July 4, 2016, in Hawthorne, California, a male driver entered a DUI checkpoint manned by officers from the CHP and Hawthorne Police Department. The driver stopped as required and rolled his window three-quarters of the way down, even going so far as to hand his driver's license to a waiting patrol officer. What happened next to the sober and cooperative young man is beyond comprehension in the supposed land of the free and the home of the brave.

Officers determined to put a match to the Constitution ordered the driver to roll his window all the way down. He refused. So the freedom-killing minions in law enforcement enacted their contingency plan, put in place for this very reason.

Goetz and obedient order-follower.

Waiting in the wings just a short distance away was a flatbed tow truck. With the discipline of a soldier on parade, the tow truck driver was summoned and the car winched aboard with the driver and passenger still seated inside the car.

Now isolated and surrounded, a Hawthorne police officer, under the watchful eye of Police Lieutenant Ty Goetz, aimed his pistol at the driver's head as they waited for the tow truck driver to unlock the door with a slim jim. The men were forced out and onto the ground for handcuffing.

The driver was jailed for "failure to comply with the rules of a DUI checkpoint" and "failure to obey a lawful order". His car was impounded and the passenger left to fend for himself on the dark and dangerous streets of central Los Angeles.

Lieutenant Goetz said after the arrest that, although the law does not require a driver to roll the window all the way down or submit to a field sobriety test, things would nevertheless "end up bad" [sic] for those who refused to cooperate.

Lieutenant Goetz, you and your jack-booted order-followers are a [expletive] stain on humanity. Especially you, Goetz.

Rutherford County, Tennessee Sheriff's Department

At another Fourth of July DUI checkpoint, this time in Rutherford County, Tennessee, a 21-year-old male driver was greeted by Sheriff's Deputy A. J. Ross. Deputy Ross did everything wrong, including yelling at the young man and lying about the law. All because the driver did not roll the window down far enough to suit Deputy Ross. He was furious that the young man had the gall to assert his constitutional rights.

What came next was law enforcement's ultimate form of retaliation: a canine officer walked a "trained" drug dog around the car. As a surprise to exactly nobody, the dog allegedly displayed behavior that indicated the possibility of drugs and/or narcotics being inside the young man's car.

Deputy Ross proceeded to rifle through the car in a vain attempt to locate illegal drugs. It was while he was searching underneath the driver's seat that Deputy Ross said to another sheriff's deputy, "He's perfectly innocent and knows his rights. He knows what the Constitution says." That was when the deputies spotted a camera laying on the front passenger seat. It captured every word and every image, including the "Oh no!" moment when the deputies realized they were being recorded.

Deputy Ross had to release the sober and very humble young man from custody after the search turned up empty; humble enough to forgo filing a formal complaint against the idiot deputy. A few months later, a smiling Ross received the prestigious "Rutherford County Sheriff's Deputy of the Year Award". Congratulations and Happy Birthday, America!

Welcome to our nation's most recent edition of "A Brave New World", where innocent motorists are funneled into a government DUI checkpoint and held at gunpoint in the interest of public safety. What's next? Being held hostage at a checkpoint because someone from a different country broke the law? That could never happen in America!

Oh, yes it can. Say hello to the United States Border Patrol, the most dysfunctional and tyrannical group of constitutional misfits to wear a badge; Lieutenants Michelle "It Sucks To Be You" Loomis and Ty "Oberster Gesetzeshüter" Goetz being the most notable exceptions.

CHAPTER NINETEEN

A Simple Question?

Q: What is the difference between malignant cancer and the
average Border Patrol agent?
A: Only one is honest about their intentions.

The following declaration can be found on the U.S.
Customs and Border Protection website:

ETHOS

Our shared identity, beliefs and aspirations...

We are the guardians of our Nation's borders

We are America's frontline

We safeguard the American homeland at and beyond our borders

We protect the American people against terrorists and the instruments of terror

We steadfastly enforce the laws of the United States while fostering our Nation's economic security through lawful international trade and travel

We serve the American people with vigilance, integrity, and professionalism

We don't believe any of this!

United States Customs and Border Protection conduct so-called "immigration checkpoints" along America's highways and byways, up to one hundred miles inland from the southern and northern borders with Mexico and Canada, respectively. Two-thirds of the U.S. population - roughly 220 million people - live within the 100-mile zone.

"Answer the [expletive] question!"

Innocent travelers are forced to stop at every checkpoint they encounter and asked if they are an American citizen. "It's a simple question," the agent is trained to say, "just answer the question and you'll be on your way."

The Government does not "ask" questions, simple or otherwise. At immigration checkpoints, travelers reluctant to answer the citizenship question are likely to have spike strips placed in front of their tires. Agents will quickly surround the vehicle, all the while ordering the driver to pull into a secondary inspection area for further inquiry into their citizenship status. (Only recently have Border Patrol agents begun to conduct random "transportation checks" of bus and train passengers. In Maine, agents were told "Happy hunting!" before they had even stepped foot onto a bus or train.)

What, then, if one simple question were to be followed by a second simple question; which is followed by a third, then a fourth simple question? Or, as was the case with a military veteran, seventeen simple questions? The only way a person can resist this type of creeping tyranny is to not answer the first question.

There is another, lesser-known problem that travelers face at immigration checkpoints. Local travelers are forced to go through area checkpoints sometimes twice a day, day after day. How many times does a local traveler have to answer the citizenship question before border agents stop asking the question under the threat of violence? A simple question, is it not?

Almost to a person, the agents who staff these checkpoints become immediately hostile when travelers assert their right not to answer the citizenship question. Multiple on-line videos have exposed and documented the unconstitutional behavior of border agents, including pulling people out of their cars and placing them in handcuffs.

In what may amount to the ultimate betrayal of the rule of law, travelers are being detained until they can prove, to the satisfaction of the agents, that they are an American citizen. An American citizen has to validate their right to be an American citizen, to a government agent who couldn't care less about the citizen's God-given right to be an American citizen.

> The evidence is incontrovertible:
> Border Patrol agents are
> depriving American citizens of
> their constitutional rights because
> SOMEONE FROM A DIFFERENT
> COUNTRY broke the law.

The evidence is incontrovertible: Border Patrol agents are depriving American citizens of their constitutional rights because SOMEONE FROM A DIFFERENT COUNTRY broke the law. Mr. President and Dishonorable Attorney General, why have you not put a stop to this unconstitutional practice?

There is another way Border Patrol agents can extract their pound of flesh from innocent travelers who dare challenge their authority. That is by walking a drug dog around the vehicle under the pretext of searching for "drugs, human bodies, or currency".

What happened to the original intent of the checkpoint, which was to quiz travelers as to their citizenship status? Immigration checkpoints are not just about checking into a traveler's citizenship status. It is mostly a ruse to allow the Border Patrol to perform drug interdiction.

It is interesting how often the drug dog "alerts" - scratching at a particular location on the vehicle or by sitting down - to the presence of illegal contraband when the vehicle is operated by a traveler who refused to answer the agent's one simple question. Because of rogue Border Patrol agents, the traveler's Fourth Amendment rights are gone. Agents now "own" the vehicle under the pretext of probable cause to search. Innocent travelers will be detained indefinitely as rogue agents tear the vehicle apart looking for phantom contraband.

For those interested, the case law the agents are abusing to search the vehicle without a search warrant or the voluntary consent of the traveler is called the "Carroll Doctrine". When performed by an honest law enforcement officer, a "Carroll" search is rarely abused. When performed by an oathbreaker with the Border Patrol, a Carroll search will almost always be abused.

Why is the abuse of a probable cause search for contraband inside a motor vehicle so incredibly dangerous, when conducted by corrupt police officers? Because, under the scope of a Carroll search, if the item or object that initiated the search can fit, it can be searched. This would include locked containers and the trunk.

Meaning, an officer cannot legally search the ashtray in hopes of finding an illegal elephant; however, what if the item or object that initiated the search were a smell? What then? How is the traveler supposed to contest the search when the probable cause to search was predicated on something so blatantly intangible as a smell? The answer is, they cannot.

On the night of April 14, 2009, at a Border Patrol immigration checkpoint near Yuma, Arizona, a mob of nearly a dozen officers from at least two law enforcement agencies ordered a driver to step from his car after a drug dog supposedly alerted to the presence of contraband. The driver dared to ask questions, so the enraged agents smashed in both side windows and tased the driver from two angles for nearly ten seconds. He was dragged screaming from his car and body-slammed onto the asphalt roadway, where his face was severely lacerated by shards of broken glass from the window.

Handcuffed and bleeding from the nose and forehead, the driver was moved to the Border Patrol's on-site trailer to await the arrival of paramedics; where it would take eleven stitches to close the wound to his forehead. As the man sat alone in the trailer, Border Patrol agents laughed and told jokes. This would explain why Border Patrol agents are five times more likely to be arrested for serious crimes than law enforcement officers in general.

No contraband was found inside the car, unsurprisingly, and the driver was acquitted on the charges of obstructing a roadway and refusing to obey a lawful order. Without getting too far into the weeds on the subject, the canine handler testified at a preliminary hearing that he had never been provided with a copy of the Border Patrol's policy on the use of trained canines at immigration check-points. Without the benefit of the policy, the agent was free to use the dog however he saw fit.

During the same preliminary hearing, an Administrative Lieutenant testified that although the Border Patrol does indeed have an internal policy on the use of trained canines, it was not at liberty to disclose its contents. This reluctance to disclose the canine policy included denying access to the driver's defense counsel, a direct violation of the man's constitutional rights.

Incredibly, the Judge sided with the Border Patrol and refused to grant defense counsel full and unfettered access to the policy. From a layman's perspective, failing to disclose the policy meant there was effectively no policy whatsoever on the use of trained canines at immigration checkpoints, or anywhere else the Border Patrol uses canines in the performance of their duties.

What did a later review of the on-site surveillance footage show? It revealed that the handler had the dog perform only a cursory sniff of the left rear quarter-panel of the car.

Government obfuscation notwithstanding, what legal obligation do travelers have if they were to encounter an immigration checkpoint? In summary, the courts have ruled that immigration checkpoints are a minimal intrusion into a person's Fourth Amendment expectation of privacy. Agents are allowed to ask the immigration question, as well as instruct travelers to move to a secondary inspection area for further inquiry into their citizenship status.

However, agents cannot compel travelers to answer the citizenship question. Nor can they detain travelers in a secondary area for more than five minutes (no more "I have all day" nonsense from border agents). Any other demand made of the traveler not otherwise compelled by suspected criminal activity is unconstitutional.

For decades, the United States has been experiencing the largest non-military invasion in human history. The main reason is our porous borders. Border Patrol agents claim to be overwhelmed by the mass of humanity seeking a better life in the United States. If this were true, why is Customs and Border Protection conducting immigration checkpoints up to one hundred miles inland from our borders with Mexico and Canada? Are they not wasting valuable resources such as manpower and other important assets to operate these checkpoints?

My advice to Customs and Border Protection agents would be to either do it the right way or move your "assets" back to the borders, where they belong.

CHAPTER TWENTY

In the United States of America...*

...innocent citizens are being harassed; detained; hand-cuffed; arrested; pepper-sprayed; struck by batons; tased; jailed; placed in a coma; having their arms broken; having their necks and heads broken; having their lives ruined; AND NEEDLESSLY LOSING THEIR LIVES AT THE HANDS OF OATHBREAKERS IN AND FOR:

- State of South Dakota for all the things I did wrong as an officer

- Sioux Falls, South Dakota for exercising free speech

- Gardena, California for standing next to a bicycle

- Fort Worth, Texas for standing inside one's own home

- Clay County, Missouri for being a tourist

- Beaver County, Oklahoma for public photography

- Madison, Alabama for going on a walk

- New York City for not paying taxes on cigarettes

- Independence, Missouri for being a 17-year-old driver

- Glendale, Arizona for being an innocent passenger

- Prairie View, Texas for not using a turn signal

- Corvallis, Oregon for riding a bicycle

- Dallas County, Texas for a burned-out license plate light

- Egg Harbor Township, New Jersey for flicking cigarette ash out the window

- Stockton, California for jaywalking

- Colorado Springs, Colorado for walking across the street

- Chester Township, Pennsylvania for standing on the sidewalk in front of one's own home

- Harris County, Texas for public photography

- Williams County, North Dakota for visiting a courtroom

- Weld County, Colorado for walking onto a wide-open patch of gravel

- Warren, Michigan for public photography

- Houston, Texas for public photography

- Dallas, Texas for public photography

- Greenville, Texas for public photography

- Los Angeles County, California for public photography

- Houston, Texas for public photography

- Washington, D.C. for public photography

- State of New Jersey for public photography

- Salem, Oregon for public photography

- Las Vegas, Nevada for public photography

- Denver, Colorado for public photography

- Kern County, California for public photography

- Anchorage, Alaska for public photography

- Universal City, Texas for public photography

- Bowling Green, Kentucky for public photography

- Fort Hood, Texas for public photography

- Corpus Christi, Texas for public photography

- Honolulu, Hawaii for public photography

- Des Moines, Iowa for public photography

- Lexington, Kentucky for public photography

- Pueblo, Colorado for public photography

- Southlake, Texas for public photography

- San Bernardino County, California for public photography

- Los Angeles, California for public photography

- Arlington, Virginia for public photography

- El Paso, Texas for public photography

- Pima County, Arizona for public photography

- Baton Rouge, Louisiana for public photography

- Mobile, Alabama for public photography

- Marion, Illinois for public photography

- Springfield, Oregon for public photography

- Plantation, Florida for public photography

- Glynn County, Georgia for public photography

- Sacramento, California for public photography

- Pevely, Missouri for holding the police accountable

- Colorado Springs, Colorado for public photography

- Tampa, Florida for public photography

- South Tucson, Arizona for exercising free speech

- Chapel Hill, North Carolina for exercising free speech

- Colorado Springs, Colorado for exercising free speech

- Comal County, Texas for exercising free speech

- State of Kentucky for exercising free speech

- Columbia County, Florida for exercising free speech

- Carey, Ohio for exercising free speech

- Fort Pierce, Florida for exercising free speech

- Royse City, Texas for exercising free speech

- Sheboygan, Wisconsin for exercising free speech

- Sherwood, Arkansas for exercising free speech

- Moultrie, Georgia for exercising free speech

- Fort Worth, Texas for exercising free speech

- Huntsville, Alabama for exercising free speech

- Little Rock, Arkansas for listening to the police

- Effingham County, Georgia for using a cell phone responsibly

- Austin, Texas for holding the police accountable

- Little Elm, Texas for failing to obey an unlawful order

- Prichard, Alabama for public photography

- Los Angeles County, California for holding the police accountable

- State of New Jersey for not answering a question

- Lenawee County, Michigan for pretty much everything

- Colorado Springs, Colorado for parking while black

- San Bernardino County, California for being an innocent passenger

- Kingsland, Georgia for public photography

- State of Rhode Island for being an innocent passenger

- Hibbing, Minnesota for public photography

- Walker, Louisiana for public photography

- Cranston, Rhode Island for public photography

- LaPorte, Texas for public photography

- West Des Moines, Iowa for canvassing voters while black

- Greer, South Carolina for public photography

- Cook County, Illinois for public photography

- Prince William County, Virginia for public photography

- Los Angeles, California for driving sober

- Hawthorne, California for driving sober

- Rutherford County, Tennessee for driving sober

- United States of America for being an American citizen

- United States of America for merely existing

To follow in Chapter 21:
- Boulder, Colorado for picking up trash while black

- Colorado Springs, Colorado for driving while black

- Taylor, Michigan for driving while black

- Alpharetta, Georgia for questioning signing a ticket while black

- Milwaukee, Wisconsin for parking while black

- Hammond, Indiana for riding in a car while black

- Baywatch, Texas for parking while black

*While nowhere near the size and scope of the Battle of Okinawa, or the magnitude of the slaughter of Union troops after just one-half day of fighting at Cold Harbor, the 36-day Battle of Iwo Jima during WWII was no less bloody for the 60,000 Marines who waded ashore. During the five-week campaign to wrest control of the island from the Imperial Japanese Army, nearly 7,000 Marines were killed and 19,000 more were wounded. Many of the young Marines died in agonizing pain, alone with their guts spilled out or their limbs blown off, screaming for their mothers to take them away from a godforsaken Pacific island 7,000 miles from home. How dare oathbreakers render meaningless the Marines' ultimate sacrifice; and all the rest who gave their last full measure for freedom.

HOW DARE THEY.

CHAPTER TWENTY-ONE

Racism in Law Enforcement

Boulder, Colorado Police Department

On the afternoon of March 1, 2019, a black college student was observed by Officer John Smiley standing on the sidewalk in front of a somewhat trendy multi-level dorm complex. Acting of his own volition, the white police officer used a simple "No Trespassing" sign posted at the rear of the complex as reasonable suspicion of the crime of trespass, then attempted to detain the man under the alleged authority of a Terry Stop.

WTH?

Without so much as a cursory introduction, Smiley engaged the young man in meaningless conversation before saying (with an annoying uplift to his voice), "I saw you sitting on the rear deck earlier. I'm just checking to make sure you have a right to be here. That's all."

Clearly baffled by the remark, the young man nevertheless handed Smiley his student ID. A generic-style college ID is not what Smiley wanted. Smiley wanted something with the young man's name, address, and date of birth; information normally found on a person's freedom papers.

"What unit are you in?" Smiley asked, referring to the young man's apartment number at the complex. Now beginning to sense the true intent behind Smiley's intrusive line of questioning, the man answered, "I don't think I have to actually tell you that." Smiley was undeterred by the student's lack of cooperation. "I need to see something that has your address and date of birth on it," Smiley said determinedly.

How would the young man's date of birth have proved where he lived? Smiley's intent lay bare: he wanted the student's date of birth to run a warrant check. It is what motivated Smiley to confront the young man in the first place, using the manufactured crime of trespass as reasonable suspicion to detain and demand his ID. No longer was it a question of if the contact would escalate, but of when and how far the contact would escalate.

Now clearly upset, the young man turned his back to Smiley and resumed picking up trash from the boulevard. He had no sooner turned his back when Smiley threatened him with a charge of "obstructing an investigation". "It's a jailable offense!" Smiley gulped. Smiley, a 14-year veteran police officer, followed the student around to the side of the complex. He stopped and reached for the mic clipped to his uniform shirt. It was a classic displacement activity that was about to be followed by Smiley lying to dispatch regarding the true nature of the contact.

"Subject is failing to comply!" Smiley told dispatch. "He's not sitting down and has some kind of blunt object in his hand!" He was referring to the simple hand-operated EZ Reacher and Grabber the student was using to pick up miscellaneous debris from the ground. Smiley further escalated the situation by repeatedly threatening to tase the college student for failing to obey his lawful order to sit down.

There were now seven Boulder police officers en route, all running with lights and sirens to help a fellow officer who said he was being threatened by an "uncooperative subject" wielding a "blunt object" of some kind.

213

What ensued was a 20-minute standoff at the rear of the complex where the young black man found himself surrounded by eight white police officers, each holding a weapon of some kind. Smiley had his pistol out and was holding the weapon at the "low ready" position.

The standoff ended after a sergeant spoke with two residents of the complex, who were able to confirm the student's identity. "Give him his ID back and we're outta here," the Sergeant instructed Officer Smiley.

Boulder Police Officer John Smiley retired shortly after the encounter. For his effort, Smiley received a $70,000 severance package.

Colorado Springs, Colorado Police Department

African-American brothers Ryan and Benjamin Brown were traveling through a predominantly white neighborhood on their way home when they were pulled over by Patrol Officers David Nelson and Allison Detweiler. Patrol Sergeant Steven Biscaro arrived a short while later. All three officers were white.

What follows is an excerpt from the ACLU's April 20, 2017 Press Release describing the incident in greater detail, along with the decision by the City of Colorado Springs to settle a lawsuit filed on behalf of the Browns by the ACLU:

"DENVER - The City of Colorado Springs has agreed to pay $212,000 to settle a racial profiling lawsuit brought by the ACLU of Colorado, alleging that Ryan and Benjamin Brown were pulled over because of their race, (assaulted), handcuffed, searched, and detained at gunpoint and taser point, all without legal justification."

"...Brown filed a complaint (after the incident) with CSPD. He received a brief boilerplate letter in June 2015 informing him that the Department had conducted a 'complete and thorough' investigation into the incident and concluded that the officers' conduct was 'justi-fied, legal, and proper.'" END OF NEWS RELEASE.

The Colorado Springs Police Department demonstrated once again the depth of corruption that is the thin blue line.

Taylor, Michigan Police Department

Short of shooting the man, the indefensible actions of a Taylor police officer during an April 2016 traffic stop - which was anything but routine - is one of the most senseless acts of violence by police officers toward an innocent driver that I am aware of. All Officer Vines had to do to keep the situation from escalating was answer Calvin Jones' one simple question at the beginning of the contact: "Why'd you pull me over?" Officer Vines refused to answer the question, despite being asked at least a half-dozen times.

Vines' reluctance to answer the question was because he knew full well there was no legitimate reason for making the stop. In his haste to pull Jones over, Officer Vines had failed to give himself enough time to manufacture a reason. So he chose to bluff his way through, hoping the still-unidentified driver would either admit to not having a valid driver's license or make some other self-incriminating remark.

Had Jones handed over the requested license and vehicle documents, which he was required to surrender by law, what Vines probably intended was to walk back to his cruiser and run Jones' driver's license information through dispatch. This would have given Vines time to fabricate a lie. Then, as a tactic intended to justify the stop and cover his backside, Vines would have almost certainly issued Jones only a verbal warning. This is another game oathbreakers like to play.

There were other clues Vines was up to no good. For instance, he had no problem threatening to arrest Jones for not providing the requested documents. Nor when he used Jones' reluctance to intimate that he was driving with a suspended driver's license.

Neither of these alleged crimes would have explained why Vines pulled Jones over. Vines would have had to articulate reasonable suspicion of crime BEFORE he made the stop. The only thing Vines told Jones prior to the violence headed Jones' way was that he was conducting an "investigatory stop", without specifying the crime he was allegedly investigating.

Lacking reasonable suspicion or probable cause of a crime, Vines had essentially positioned himself to investigate whatever he wanted to investigate. This would include being able to investigate whether Jones had heeded his mother's advice to always wear clean underwear, or if Jones had paid attention during "Lower Lip Louie's" 7th-grade math class.

Jones was not playing along and had called Vines' bluff. So Vines did what every oathbreaker does when the mess they created goes south. He keyed the mic on his portable radio and requested backup to help bring the "uncooperative occupant" under control.

Soon the gang had assembled and the officers "gloved-up" in anticipation of the upcoming violence, because experience told them that the driver's head might bleed afterward. "Be prepared!" as they say in the Boy Scouts.

Officer Vines took the lead. He grabbed the top of the driver's window and pulled with such force that it shattered the window, only he pulled so hard that he landed flat on his back and was nearly run over by the driver of a minivan.

With the speed of Hermes from Greek mythology, Officer Vines and his gang descended upon Jones. Pandemonium erupted as the gang attacked Jones inside the car, finally able to drag the 26-year-old black man out and slam him onto the asphalt roadway.

Over the course of the next several minutes, as the pummeled Jones was left gasping for air in the middle of the street, not a single officer bothered to tell him why he had been stopped or the reason he had been arrested. Neither were his African-American wife - likewise assaulted by Vines - nor a young African-American passenger, told why they were placed in chains and headed for a cage.

What Vines and the other Taylor police officers did that day neither served nor protected anyone. Their actions were born not out of malfeasance, but out of a descent into racial madness.

Alpharetta, Georgia Police Department
In Alpharetta, the arrest of a driver led to an officer having to resign from the police force. It was an incident captured on video by a patrolman's dashboard camera, which showed Patrol Officer James Legg (with the heavily-tattooed forearms) screaming obscenities. "You're not in charge!" Legg yelled. "Shut the [expletive] up and get out of the car!"

What led to the encounter was the driver's intransigence. Confused over whether signing the ticket - for crossing over the centerline of the road - was an admission of guilt, the driver asked to speak with a supervisor.

Officer Legg ordered the driver to step out of the car. When the driver refused, Officer Legg and five more brave and burly oathbreakers plucked the driver forcibly from the car - Click! - as the terrified driver cried out in pain.

Although he regretted using profanity during the incident, Legg said he believed he had acted appropriately when he chained and caged the 65-year-old African-American grandmother.

Milwaukee, Wisconsin Police Department

On a frigid night in January 2018, Police Officer Erik Andrade contacted 22-year-old Sterling Brown for parking across two handicap parking spots outside a Walgreens store on the south side of Milwaukee. It was two o'clock in the morning when Andrade pulled up next to Brown's car. Except for Andrade's police cruiser, Brown's car was the only other car in the entire parking lot. Officer Andrade was acting of his own volition, with no involvement by Walgreens staff whatsoever.

> **It shouldn't require an incident involving a professional athlete to draw attention to the fact that vulnerable people in our communities have experienced similar, and even worse, treatment."**
>
> —Milwaukee Bucks Statement

Rude from the start, Andrade escalated the contact with Brown over an infraction that should have been handled with a verbal warning. When a respectful Brown questioned his handling of the situation, Andrade reached for the mic clipped to his uniform shirt and requested backup. Six Milwaukee police officers responded to Andrade's radio call for help.

Seven white police officers, each carrying a high-capacity pistol and the ubiquitous yellow-handled Taser, were arrayed against a lone black man standing helplessly in a Walgreens parking lot. Numerical superiority and too-easily-deployed Tasers meant Sterling Brown was about to be attacked by seven ramped-up Milwaukee police officers.

"Hands! Show us your hands!" the officers barked as they surrounded Brown. Most appalling was the expression of hatred sculpted into the faces of the officers. They failed to see Brown's fallibility, as they themselves are fallible.

It was quick and brutal. Brown was jumped and slammed to the ground. "Taser! Taser! Taser!" echoed through the chilly early morning air. One of the officers intentionally stepped on Brown's left ankle, potentially ending the young man's pro-basketball career with the hometown Milwaukee Bucks.

Sterling Brown was arrested for "obstruction" and "resisting arrest". Both charges were quickly dismissed. Officer Andrade was later fired for leaving a racially insensitive post on his Facebook page. Given the MPD's history of racism, it will happen again to another innocent person of color. Just give it time.

Looking back, it would have been impossible for a handicapped person to reach the parking spots that Brown was beaten over. Not because Brown's car was in the way, but because of the endless sea of police cars that were in the way. As I said, it should have been handled with a verbal warning.

Hammond, Indiana Police Department

In September 2015, a female driver and male passenger were pulled over for not wearing their seatbelts. For some reason, it was the passenger who drew the attention of officers. "He needs to come out of the vehicle. I don't know who he is, and I'm a little nervous," a sergeant told the growing cluster of police officers.

Oathbreakers have ice-cold demeanors and the Hammond police officers were no exception. They each had lifeless eyes, hardened hearts, and an abject hatred for a fellow human being. As if to prove the point, the same sergeant hurled insults at the man after he requested to speak with a supervisor. "Look at my shoulder, dumb [expletive]! I got the bars!"

A Shift Commander finally arrived, but instead of using civility to de-escalate the situation, he used the butt-end of a PR-24 side-handle baton to smash out the passenger window. Stunned into submission by a Taser, the man was dragged from the car and handcuffed. Officers went on to charge the man with "resisting an officer" and "failure to come to the aid of an officer". No charge was filed for the predicate crime of not wearing a seatbelt.

A spokesperson for the Police Department released the following statement shortly after the man's arrest: "The Hammond Police Officers were at all times acting in the interest of officer safety and in accordance with Indiana law."

So, it was apparently fine for a gang of white police officers to beat up a black man for not wearing a seatbelt, as long as it was done in the name of officer safety? Or, were the officers so concerned about the man getting hurt for not wearing a seatbelt, that they decided to hurt the man to teach him a lesson about not wearing a seatbelt?

Baywatch, Texas Police Department

A black man was spotted sitting alone in a car parked in the lot of a well-lit convenience store. How long is too long for a lone black man to be parked in a convenience store parking lot? Long enough to make him a "suspicious person" in the eyes of two white Baywatch police officers.

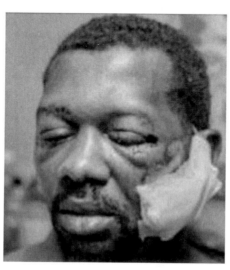

A so-called "suspicious" black man sitting inside a car was only minutes away from being beaten nearly to death, the victim of racial profiling. If only he had known his constitutional rights.

Had he known his rights, the man would have understood that he had no legal obligation to let the officers search his car. This is why legal scholars call it a "consent search" (for the reader's benefit, officers are legally required to use the word "search" in their request for consent). That, and the man had made the mistake of thinking too hard.

This was probably the first time he had faced something so unexpected: two police officers emerging from the darkness of night, asking to search his car. What would the officers think if he were to say no? That he must have something to hide? This is where so many citizens go awry, worrying about what the police might think. Instead, he foolishly surrendered his Fourth Amendment rights and granted the officers consent to search his car.

There was still time to withdraw consent before the officers found something that could be construed as contraband. His window of opportunity slammed shut when, unbeknownst to the man, an officer discovered a baggie of assorted pills - which were lawfully-prescribed antibiotics - in the console and had given his partner the high sign.

Suddenly and without warning the pair attacked the man, pushing him face-down over the hood of the car. "Stop resisting!" both officers yelled at a black man who knew only that two white police officers were determined to place him back in chains. Despite his many pleas, neither officer would tell the man why he was being arrested. The beating began in earnest when the man "passively" resisted the officers' efforts to place him in handcuffs.

During the subsequent beating, the man was punched, kicked, and tased too many times to count. Next came multiple baton strikes to his legs and torso, as he screamed and writhed on the ground. Sirens screamed in the distance as the first of many backup officers arrived. Finally, officers were able to get the "suspicious" black man handcuffed and under some semblance of control.

Incredibly, one of the charges filed against the man was felony assault on a police officer after an officer claimed he had been "scratched" during the lopsided melee. In hindsight, how were the man's injuries not partially self-inflicted, the price he paid for not knowing his constitutional rights?

There was a time when I believed people of color were overstating their problems with the police. Now I believe their problems with the police have been understated. American jurisprudence has treated people of color differently. They have been left out and left behind, denied justice by the "system".

This is why people of color, mainly African-Americans, have reason to fear the police. This is why I believe the best remedy is to do to the officers what they did to the victim. This is why Americans need to put down their cell phones and video game controllers and learn their constitutional rights. Citizens who stumble through life oblivious of their rights means the Constitution no longer exists.

Racism is symptomatic of the on-going moral decay that permeates the law enforcement profession in America. Those who would jump to the defense of the police - asserting the increased police presence is a necessary consequence of higher crime rates in minority neighborhoods - are failing to see my point. This is about racial profiling being wrong regardless of the circumstances.

Citizens should not be so naive to think that racist cops will confine their illegal and unconstitutional behavior to the "hood". A racist cop will check neither their bigotry nor their contempt for the public just because they have moved their patrol efforts to the "other side of the tracks".

Thanks to racist cops, good cops are accused of racism too. It is an unsettling charge. First, it is virtually impossible to disprove (i.e. a "Russell's Teapot"); and second, an otherwise lawful interaction can take on a new and dangerous dynamic, one where common sense can be overruled by raw emotion.

Being accused of racism happened twice during my career. Each accusation was unsettling.

CHAPTER TWENTY-TWO

Ferguson, Missouri

How much worse it must be for a non-racist police offi-cer to be accused of racism after the 2014 fatal shooting of 18-year-old Michael Brown in Ferguson, Missouri. For the record, what follows is not an indictment of Michael Brown. It is to try and place the issue of racism in its proper context, as it relates to my own experience with being labeled a racist.

Michael Brown's fatal shooting by a white police officer, Darren Wilson, was ruled justifiable. In and of itself, the incident neither ignited nor renewed racial tensions in America. The smoldering embers of entrenched racial animus were fanned into a conflagration by a complicit media; academia; Hollywood; the attorney general; and a sitting president. All were quick to exploit an incident they construed as racially motivated.

They were so easily fooled by the young man who was with Michael Brown at the time Brown committed a strong-arm robbery and, later, when Brown was shot and killed by Wilson. Racial mayhem was unleashed upon America with four words: "Hands up, don't shoot."

It was all a lie.

"Hands up, don't shoot" was not a part of the American lexicon when I was accused of being a racist. It needn't be. For decades, minority populations were inculcated with the notion that America in general, and police officers in particular, were inherently racist. A person of color could never get ahead in racist America.

It was a message rightly based on countless historical injustices; however, the way the message was conveyed devastated parts of the minority community. It reeked of defeatism and cold-heartedly convinced many minorities to stop trying to make a better life for themselves. It further convinced others not to try in the first place.

In a broad sense, the ceaseless rhetoric conflated bad officers with good officers. It encouraged those in the minority community to openly resist police authority, even when overt racism by law enforcement was lacking.

Every police contact was racially motivated, so it was claimed. Blatant criminality followed by upstanding police conduct was ignored. All that mattered was if the person were a minority and the police officer was white.

CHAPTER TWENTY-THREE

Racista Policia

My first encounter with alleged racism as a game war-den was at Wall Lake, the small lake with the big crime problem just west of Sioux Falls. The allegation of racism was the reason why an otherwise lawful contact with a person of color nearly turned into an act of violence on their part.

Old-timers might remember when the doors of the Beach House Bar and Restaurant on the south side of Wall Lake were open for business. The Beach House was situated on the far west side of the public beach, while a stone's throw to the south sat an older home ensconced in a forest of old-growth trees. Both the house and the trees are still standing, I hope.

Parked in the cooling shade under one of the massive canopies that sweltering day was me, watching the varied activities around the lake through the eyepiece of a 22-power spotting scope. "It" pulled in and parked on the driveway approach, maybe thirty feet from me. "It" was not Pennywise, the kid-killing sewer clown from the Stephen King novel by the same name. It was the arrival of four young men enjoying a summertime cruise around Wall Lake in a shiny red convertible.

Despite being parked so close to my marked patrol vehicle, not one of the men saw me. Not even a glance in my direction. Pssshhh! went a can of Budweiser beer. This was followed by two long pulls and a flick of the wrist, which sent the can over the side and into the ditch. It had taken all of fifteen seconds for one of the men sitting in the back to commit two misdemeanors in my presence.

It is said that context is everything. The only reason I was at the lake that day was to do the job that I was hired to do. Nothing more, nothing less. As for the four men in the shiny red convertible, no one forced them to drive to the lake. Nor did anyone force the men to park where they did. No one forced a rear seat passenger to crack open a beer. Nor did anyone force the rear seat passenger to pitch the can into the ditch. Everything the men did up to that point, they had done of their own free will.

As for me, I never took note of the men's ethnicities when they pulled into the driveway approach. Nor would taking note of their ethnicities have influenced my decision to write the back seat passenger a ticket for littering.

In hindsight, it would have been a much better idea had I stopped the car away from the sights and sounds of the beach. Alas, I did not, choosing to make the stop above the busy beach. The beachgoers were about to see a spectacle none would have imagined.

It started the second after I had explained what was going on and requested identification. To say he went insane would be an understatement. His behavior was so violent that I had to retreat to the front of my truck.

He was jumping up and down on the back seat like it was a trampoline, all the while screaming "RACIST!" at the top of his lungs. He screamed "RACIST!" over and over while continuing to jump up and down on the seat. He eventually grew tired of screaming the same word over and over, so he switched from yelling "RACIST!" to yelling "RACISM!" over and over as he continued to use the back seat as a trampoline.

He switched again and screamed "LAWYER! I WANT A LAWYER!" over and over. "Are you done acting like a child?" I asked the crazy man jumping up and down on the back seat. "Because if you're not, I'm going to arrest you for disorderly conduct!" He stepped from the car and handed me his Florida driver's license.

The contact went well from that point on, although it was a tad bit more complicated than I am willing to reveal. Chalk it up to the vagaries of wearing a badge!

By the way, the man did not accuse me of being a racist because of anything I had said or done. Nor was his anger a byproduct of being falsely accused of a crime. He accused me of being a racist because I was Caucasian and he was Hispanic. Funny thing is, it was only after he told me that I realized he was Hispanic.

CHAPTER TWENTY-FOUR

Reggie, Victor, and Bobby

A picture-perfect autumn afternoon in late October is the kind of day that makes being a game warden the best job on the planet. With the pheasant season open, it was the best kind of day to venture into the countryside to check pheasant hunters.

It was while I was sitting at my desk at the Sioux Falls Regional Office preparing to go out on patrol that the telephone rang. There was a gruff male voice on the other end of the line, and he sounded upset.

His complaint was straightforward: there were two men hunting pheasants on his land without permission. He said they were too far away to note their physical appearance. On the other hand, the men were plenty close enough to see they were armed. That fact convinced the Hartford-area farmer to get hold of a game warden, rather than try to handle things on his own. He jotted down the van's license plate number and made a phone call to the Sioux Falls office.

Trespassing to hunt or fish is one of the few game violations with a "victim", so to speak. It was the farmer who was the "victim" by virtue of his property rights being violated. Even so, there would be no follow-up investigation without absolute assurance from the farmer that he wanted to proceed with a charge of trespass and that he would be willing to testify in court. The farmer asked me to proceed and assured me he would testify against the two men at trial if necessary.

My investigation took me to a modest home on Cleveland Avenue in central Sioux Falls, where I had hoped to find the van parked either on the street or in the driveway. Unfortunately, my luck finding the van was as fleeting as the van was itself. Neither were anywhere in sight.

So I decided to do a quick "knock and talk" and leave my contact information with whoever was home. The well-laid plan fell apart as soon as the older gentleman answered the door. Not one word. He just stood and glared at me.

What the man said right after I had introduced myself and explained the reason for the visit gave me pause. Had he implied what I think he had just implied, I asked myself? He surely had.

"Reggie, Victor, and Bobby".

How dare he say something like that! This man knew nothing about me or what was in my heart. How could he know that I had been born and raised on the west side of Philadelphia, at a time when the country was being ripped apart by the Vietnam War and the birth pangs of an awakening civil rights movement?

How could he possibly know the number of times my twin brother and I were assailed by some of the older kids in the neighborhood? The names we were called, or the threats that were made, only because we had friends who were "different" from theirs?

Then came an epiphany, after I realized I knew no more about this man's life than he knew about mine.

It was with certainty that I knew the investigation was over. That I knew I would ask the farmer to reconsider his decision to proceed with trespass charges against the two young men. He did reconsider his complaint and the matter was formally resolved with two written warnings for trespass.

His reaction to my presence that afternoon was no doubt a byproduct of the man's encounters with other men through the years. Men whose racist inclinations could only be assuaged by self-effacing conduct on his part. How many times this must have happened for the man to say "Those are my sons, and I think I know why this is being pursued" to an officer who had been close friends with Reggie, Victor and Bobby decades earlier in Philadelphia. My friends were black, the same as the father and his two young sons.

CHAPTER TWENTY-FIVE

Once Corrupt, Always Corrupt

Corruption within the upper-level management of Game, Fish, and Parks was fairly common during my years of service. Even the passing of time cannot diminish the importance of telling these tales of intra-agency rot, for no other reason than that it may help discourage future corruption within state government.

Our journey through the cesspool of corruption begins with a supervisor from the Sioux Falls Regional Office, who helped himself to $1,000 worth of "spare" lumber from the department's maintenance shop to build a palatial dog house. He was eventually caught after word of his thievery got out, although his "punishment" was to simply replace the lumber. Disclosure: I used a sheet of green-treated plywood from the same maintenance shop to replace the rotted plywood under the front casting platform of my Lund Rebel boat. A day later there were two sheets of green-treated plywood stacked in place, where before there had been only one.

Another supervisor helped himself to an expensive piece of farm equipment from the maintenance shop in Aberdeen to use on his hobby farm. He kept the piece for several years until he received a phone call from the Pierre headquarters requesting that he return the equipment, no questions asked.

One night, several high-level administrators from the Pierre office got their pointed heads together and decided there were too many leftover deer licenses remaining, first for Bennett County, then later on for Hughes County. Both times the staff at the department's Pierre licensing office were ordered to make the unsold licenses disappear from the department's website. In doing so, the administrators had knowingly conspired to violate state law SDCL 41-2-18.1 (a non-criminal offense, since changed to an administrative rule) that specifically prohibited the department from altering ANY PART of an established big game season without first going through the emergency rules process.

What are the possible ramifications when upper-level management tinkers with an established big game season? It is prima facie evidence of managerial incompetence and violates the good-faith promise made to hunters when the seasons were set. It steals legitimate hunting opportunities from sports men and women who intended to hunt but chose not to apply during the regular license lottery due to future scheduling uncertainties.

There are hunters who know from longstanding tradition that leftover deer licenses will be available for sale and simply wait to apply, unaware that they are going to be double-crossed by upper-level management. What if a high-level administrator with a personal agenda were to sneakily alter the number and type of licenses available in a big game hunting unit? What then?

Of greater importance is the notion that once corrupt, always corrupt; that getting away with stealing one cookie from the cookie jar makes it far more likely that the bandit will raid the cookie jar again.

The five conspirators eventually confessed to the deed, with one saying flatly that they wanted to avoid the "hassle" of going through the emergency rules process. Of the five co-conspirators, it was the Director of the Wildlife Division who was the biggest fish to swim into the net. He confessed to me in an email that he had gone outside the scope of his authority - an eerily familiar phrase, aye Herr Director? - when he conspired to have the licenses pulled.

To a man, they accused me of being "selfish" for stirring the pot. Stirring the pot was selfish on my part? Being "selfish" is how I learned about the plot in the first place. It just so happens that I was one of those "double-crossed deer hunters who know from long-standing tradition that leftover deer licenses will be available for sale and simply wait to apply" guys. Knowing there were 98 deer licenses available one day and zero the next is how I found out.

In order to save face, the bosses boldly, but wrongly, asserted that they had set a legal precedent after getting away with the Bennett County fiasco. This kind of uber-strange criminal logic must be a consequence of having a Master's Degree in the biological sciences.

Although too late for Bennett County deer hunters, the unsold deer licenses for Hughes County magically reappeared on the department's website - so I was able to go deer hunting after all. Upper-level management never forgave me for stirring the pot, which was laughable seeing how it had all gotten started after two well-connected Hughes County landowners complained that they were seeing too few deer while deer hunting!

Cowardice amongst upper-level management was as common a commodity as corruption. One fall, there was talk of closing the

West River Deer Season due to the extreme fire danger brought on by several consecutive years of drought. Concerns were understandable. Unbeknownst to me, however, was the Pierre brain-trust had jumped the gun.

They had gathered together a bunch of Eager Beaver department volunteers to call every nonresident license holder and warn them not to come to South Dakota. The game commission was convening an emergency session to decide whether or not to close the West River Deer Season, so the hunters were told.

"Not to worry!" the hunters were reassured. "The vote by the game commission is merely a formality. There is no doubt that the commission will vote to close the season, and y'all can take that to the bank!"

So it was to the bank the nonresident deer hunters went, having had to take out loans to cover all the debt they had incurred after canceling thousands of dollars worth of airline flights, rental cars, and hotel reservations. Adding insult to injury was when the hunters learned that the game commission had voted not to close the West River Deer Season.

Worse than the thought of lost hunting opportunities was the economic hardship it would have brought to countless communities throughout western South Dakota. Their economies relied heavily upon the revenue generated by out-of-state hunters.

"Gosh, where is everyone?" I asked myself as I strolled into the office shortly after learning of the debacle. "I seem to be the only program administrator in the office today!" That's because I WAS the only program administrator in the office that day.

Nearly every employee involved with Operation F.U.B.A.R. went A.W.O.L. for the day, leaving me high and dry to deal with the soul-searching phone calls from a dozen or more recently bankrupted deer hunters. When all was said and done, it was just another G.F.P. S.N.A.F.U.!

This brings us to the twisted tale of corruption involving a notorious big-wig from Pierre. Hiding behind the flimsiest of excuses, for five years he allowed a buddy from Washington D.C. to secretly use his home address in Pierre to procure resident hunting and fishing licenses. Their crimes only surfaced after the buddy killed an elk in the Black Hills and then tried to drop it off for processing at a local locker plant.

Somehow an employee of the locker plant caught on and reported the scheme to the local game warden, who opened a criminal investigation with the assistance of a Special Agent with the United States Fish and Wildlife Service. Angry and in a panic, the big-wig called the warden and threatened to fire him, which the big-wig later said was motivated by what he believed to be the officer's lack of professional courtesy. Meaning, the officer should have told the big-wig he was the subject of a criminal investigation.

His D.C. buddy boy got away with his crimes in the end, as did the no-account big-wig. His after-the-fact "punishment" was to embark upon a statewide intra-agency apology tour under orders from itty-bitty Governor Marion.

In March 1990, I destroyed three discs in my lower back while trying to load a roadkill deer into the bed of my truck. As devastating as the injury was, there were three simple-minded supervisors assigned to the Sioux Falls Regional Office who only made things worse.

The first simpleton refused my request to suspend my roadkill deer disposal duties, at least until I was able to walk upright again.

Possessing neither reason nor compassion, the close-minded simpleton let loose a string of profanity and ordered me to continue picking up roadkill deer, with the unrealistic caveat that I bring someone along to help.

The second simpleton was an overly-competitive fair-haired child with a hair-trigger temper and squeaky voice. He knowingly falsified information about the incident in a report he sent to state worker's compensation. In the report, he asserted that I would not stop picking up roadkill deer even though I had been told repeatedly to stop. Whatever. A concerned employee with worker's compensation in Pierre familiar with my case was generous enough to provide me a copy of the letter, which I still have.

By sending the letter via the Post Office, "Squeak" had committed the crime of mail fraud. As soon as the letter was opened by someone at worker's compensation, "Squcak" had committed the crime of filing a false report with the state. Obviously what mattered most to "Squeak the unindicted felon" was covering his backside and trying to stave off a possible lawsuit brought against himself and the department.

Which brings me to the third simpleton, otherwise known as Al Capone. He spoke with a squeaky voice, too. Al lifted my spirits within just days of the injury by calling me stupid. "You can't sue the state!" Al chortled. "You'd have to sue yourself for your own stupidity for the way you picked up the deer!" (To make clear the depth of his professional depravity, Al got angry after failing to make a case against a suspected deer poacher. As a way to retaliate for his failure, Al called the poacher's wife anonymously and yelled, "KEEP YOUR HUSBAND AWAY FROM MY WIFE!" In yet another incident, Al got angry at two officers for messing up a deer decoy operation during the East River Deer Season. Instead of berating the officers,

Al unleashed his wrath on me as I was standing on the road that snakes its way to the far southeast corner of the Beaver Creek Nature Area. This was after Al had chewed my [expletive] undeservedly that morning. After Al let me have it, he spun out with his SUV and pelted me with rocks and gravel kicked up by the rear tires.)

Did I happen to mention that Al was nuts?

Then simple-minded Al and the other two simple-minded supervisors put the screws to me again.

Simpleton Al got things started by initiating a confrontation with a man who had stopped by the Sioux Falls office, confused over where to pay a ticket. "Look, if you wanna come down here and be a smart [expletive]!" Al squealed amidst other personal insults. "Smart [expletive]?" the man replied. "Why'd you call me a smart [expletive]?"

Also realizing that Al was nuts, the man cried "I'm leaving!" and made his way to the door. Not so fast! Al went hands-on and tried to block the man's exit. He managed to sidestep Al and bolted through the front office door to freedom.

Once outside, the man fled to his car with simple-minded Al in pursuit and waving his baton in the air. Al stood on the sidewalk in front of the office - at high noon on West 10th Street - and exchanged playground pleasantries with the man. On his way back into the office, simpleton Al demolished the decorative cedar rail fence in front of the office by attempting to collapse the baton on the top rail. In a rare moment of lucidity, after he had chopped the cedar rail fence into kindling wood, Al bent down and collapsed the baton on the sidewalk.

It was just a few days later when the other two simpletons invited me to lunch at a somewhat trendy buffet-style eatery on 41st

Street. The three of us had barely sat down when the matter of our crazy-in-the-head colleague came up. I was hoping they would allow my complaint of gross misconduct to go forward, but they circled the wagons instead.

"You know how he is," the older of the two simpletons said. "We won't be able to protect you if you go after him." Message sent and received! Interestingly enough, after the verbal melee had spilled out onto the sidewalk, Squeak, the still-unindicted felon, was standing right beside me looking out the door. Apparently his comment "He's lost it!" had slipped Squeak's mind.

If that were not enough, a few days later the young man returned to pick up his fishing pole the ticketing officer had seized as evidence. Following in his wake were two Sioux Falls police officers. "He asked us to tag along," one of the police officers remarked, "because he said someone chased him with a stick the last time he was here."

Then there is the tale of the crooked Pierre administrator who knowingly obstructed an active criminal investigation involving a wildly successful professional football player. Despite his massive wealth, the pro athlete had committed numerous counts of fraud by repeatedly applying for South Dakota resident game and fish licenses, when in fact he lived in a state 1,500 miles to the east.

There is more to the story than just a crooked administrator obstructing an active criminal investigation. The cowardly crook went behind my back to give work direction to an employee who worked below me in the chain of command. He went behind my back a second time when he ordered the same employee to stand down after I had ordered the employee to re-open the investigation.

Still not done, he managed to get State Attorney General Larry Long involved. Although admittedly Larry's involvement in the legal debacle was after-the-fact and relatively minor, he nonetheless provided legal cover for the crook. Shame on you, Larry.

Perhaps worst of all was the way the crooked administrator showed favoritism to someone rich and famous, at the expense of the "little guy". So much for the equal protection clause found in the Fourteenth Amendment to the Constitution. Not surprisingly, the cowardly crook is still employed as a high-level administrator and is one of the very few people who have figured out a way to get rich working in the wildlife management profession.

Other than a momentary ding to his reputation, the NFL star (a real Patriot!) with oodles of cash was allowed to walk away from the entire ordeal unscathed. He only had to surrender his South Dakota driver's license and register his personal vehicles in his state of residence. Can anyone say "quid pro quo?"

So I implore thee remain vigilant, for in the distance comes a tempest. Trembling and powerful. Growing closer now. A brutish gang of thick black clouds and blinding blue flashes, foreshadowing chaos and violence. Closer still. Undisciplined by nature. Smothering before it life, liberty, and the pursuit of happiness. Still closer. Roiling within is the fetid stench of self-indulgence, driven by the power of greed and self-serving interests.

There! Above the din! Do you not hear it? 'Tis the deafening sound of ten million voices crying out "Obey us, for we are your masters! Give us your liberty. Give us your laughter. For we are the tools of an oppressive government. 'Tis only God may find our souls!"

"Statim corrumpere, semper corrumpere!"

CHAPTER TWENTY-SIX

Officer Discretion is Not a Four-Letter Word

*Discretion in law enforcement...is crucial to both
the functioning of the police department and to the relationship
with the public the police department serves.*
- Ethics in Law Enforcement -

One of the most disturbing statements I heard on the topic of officer discretion in law enforcement was made by a department field training officer from Sioux Falls, who said to my face, "There's no room for discretion in our field training program." His remark lay bare a fundamental flaw in the way officers are trained and confirmed why so many police agencies continue to puke out officers with one-dimensional thinking and the people skills of a pissant.

It is said that a fish rots from the head down. If an agency's field training program either implicitly or explicitly discourages officer discretion, it will default to a field training program that encourages officer indiscretion. Whatever bad voodoo arises from such willful ignorance is the fault of the rotten fish heads in upper-level management.

A field training program that fails to incorporate even the most rudimentary discussion on the application of officer discretion is derelict, mainly because officer discretion is one of the few areas where law enforcement merges fully with human dimensions. I issued two warnings for every ticket/arrest during my career and not once did I feel that I was compromising my law enforcement efforts. It was never about numbers; rather, it was about making good cases.

It was later in my career when I developed the "Compliance Continuum", a compilation of independent enforcement options available to an officer based upon the totality of the circumstances. This was followed by a "menu" of factors that defined with specificity the totality of the circumstances. These are a collection of independent variables that are available to help guide, not decide, an officer's use of discretion. It worked well for me and I believe it would work well for others, except for those officers who simply refuse to allow humanity to play a role in their decision-making process.

Compliance Continuum: public education and community outreach efforts; officer presence through high-visibility patrol; verbal warnings; written warnings; citations; arrests.

Totality of the Circumstances "Menu" (either whole or in part): the age and overall wherewithal of the offender; level of experience (hunting, fishing, etc.); level of cooperation; honesty; number of crimes committed at the time of apprehension; the seriousness of the crime(s); presence (or absence) of criminal intent; known criminal history; and acceptance of personal responsibility for their actions.

What follows is the inevitable consequence when officers choose to ignore every item on the menu.

It was the opening day of the early Canada goose season in South Dakota. A husband and wife couple had harvested two beautiful birds; one destined for the table on Thanksgiving, the other headed to a local taxidermist. What made the hunt even more memorable was the wife had finally agreed to try her hand at hunting!

Waiting for the couple to leave the field were two young game wardens, intending to check the couple for license and bag limit compliance.

There was nothing the couple needed to worry about. They had been hunting during an open season. They possessed a legal limit of geese. They had waited for legal shooting hours to start. They had permission to hunt the field. Their shotguns were plugged and only steel shotshells were in their possession.

What had started as a beautiful day turned dark and gloomy over a $2 state waterfowl stamp that was missing from the wife's hunting license.

So the two young game wardens, both of whom were recent graduates of a field training program that had no room for discretion, wrote the wife a ticket and seized her one and only Canada goose as evidence.

Understanding our humanity was an enforcement philosophy that meant nothing to two young game wardens. For the young couple on their first and last hunt together, it would have meant the world.

CHAPTER TWENTY-SEVEN

Birds of a Feather

Working the I-90 pheasant checks at the eastbound Salem rest area each fall gave me pause. Sure, we caught our fair share of poachers and there was certainly a need for the checks. For me, it was the mob mentality that bothered me the most. It quickly devolved into a ticket-writing frenzy with common sense as the most notable casualty.

Pivotal was the enforcement of the "insufficient plumage" regulation, which required that a sufficient amount of plumage be left attached to the carcasses of small game birds - such as rooster pheasants - to facilitate identification and count. Examples include an attached head, fully-feathered wing, or an attached leg (due to roosters having spurs). Since male pheasants are brightly colored and hens are not, either of the other two plumage requirements will quickly confirm that the birds are roosters.

As layers of the "golden eggs", hen pheasants are fully protected and, thus, the reason for the plumage requirements. Pheasant management in South Dakota is fairly simple and straightforward: improve pheasant habitat, protect hens, and shoot the bejesus out of roosters.

This story begins with four first-time pheasant hunters from Iowa, who stopped at the game check and were greeted by yours truly. Tired but extremely polite, the hunters milled around the back of their sedan, waiting for me to finish my inspection of licenses and game. They had removed an old cooler from the trunk and popped open the lid so I could inspect the birds. There, swimming in two inches of ice water, were nine gutted pheasant carcasses and not a feather in sight.

It had taken the hunters the better part of four days to kill thirteen birds (four were left with a taxidermist) when they could have legally taken up to forty-eight birds according to the daily limit. What some hunters might mistakenly think was a wasted trip was the hunt of a lifetime to the four young men from the Hawkeye state! Little did they know, however, that the game warden standing beside them that early pre-dawn morning had the power to ruin everything.

CHAPTER TWENTY-EIGHT

Whatchamacallits

My head on a swivel, I glanced around the parking lot on the lookout for the errant supervisor or the less-than-ambitious warden, either of whom would have gleefully written the ticket and seized the birds had they found out.

Over my dead body.

There it was, the glimmer of hope I was looking for! The birds weren't frozen. Being that the birds weren't frozen meant I would have no trouble finding the two tiny, tan and bean-shaped whatchamacallits tucked in tight near the bottom of the spine.

So I pried open the lower half of each naked carcass in search of the whatchamacallits. Low and behold, each carcass had a beautiful pair of whatchamacallits! That is how I was able to tell the birds were roosters, by their gonads!

The four young men from Iowa drove home with a cooler tucked safely inside the trunk of their older model sedan. Tucked safely inside the cooler were nine bare naked rooster pheasants, the most beautiful birds a person could have ever laid eyes on!

CHAPTER TWENTY-NINE

Charlie

Many years ago, there were two good ol' boys who wan-dered into the I-90 game check. It was just the three of us getting acquainted on the far side of the rest area parking lot, far enough from the hustle and bustle of the check it seemed as if we were all alone.

One of the good ol' boys was named Charlie, a real southern gentleman from a small town in rural Tennessee, born and raised! Charlie lived in an area thick with bobwhite quail, a sporting little critter that Charlie sorely loved to hunt. Still, in Charlie's mind, nothing could compare to hunting a smart and feisty Chinese import hundreds of miles away, in what had become Charlie's second favorite state. It was the ring-necked pheasants of South Dakota that he desired to hunt most of all!

Sadly, the relentless passing of time and the inevitable wear and tear of life had taken their toll on old Charlie. He could no longer hunt those devilish long tails the way he used to hunt them, with a joyous heart and unfettered passion. It was hunting the way it should be, tramping through the weedy grasslands and shoulder-high food plots of South Dakota.

It was after he had stepped out and started to walk that I first heard the cry. A wince, quick and sharp, followed by a second, then a third. Pain so painfully obvious, with plaintive eyes that betrayed his need of a helping hand, his pride keeping him from asking.

His business done, it was time to leave. Before Charlie left, I recall hearing the most heart-rending confession: "Just two old gentlemen on their last hunt." His words were hesitant, spoken with misty eyes and a quivering voice that betrayed a reluctant acceptance.

It was over, I realized then. It would be the memories of a hundred fields and a thousand flushes that would return Charlie to his glory days amidst the weed-infested croplands of South Dakota.

My last recollection of Charlie is watching as he rode away, sitting with stoic dignity and staring at me through the rear window of the station wagon. Charlie was staring at me from inside his wire kennel, heading home to faraway Tennessee.

CHAPTER THIRTY

A Lifelong Regret

The opening morning of the 1984 duck season found
me checking duck hunters at Buffalo Slough Game Production Area,
a state-managed public hunting area just south of Chester. My truck
was hidden beside a solid wall of bulrush and phragmites, out of
view of the primitive boat launch that sloped maybe ten feet before
disappearing into the murky waters of Skunk Creek.

It was moderately busy that chilly early-October morning. As
I recall, it was somewhere around 9:30 when the last hunters pulled
up to the launch. It was an agreeable father and son pair from Sioux
Falls. It took all of five minutes from the time we met to begin writing the worst ticket of my career.

Those were the days when the licenses required to hunt
ducks were a patchwork of state and federal stamps that had to be
signed and attached to the back of either a $2 Basic License or a
$20 Sportsman's License. One of the main advantages of buying
the Sportsman's License over the Basic License was the Sportsman's
License had the cost of most of the stamps included in the purchase

price, whereas the Basic License did not. A die-hard hunter who purchased a Basic License would have so many stamps attached to the
back that they often ran out of room!

Oddly enough, one of the requisite stamps to hunt ducks at the
time was a $5 Pheasant Restoration Stamp. It was a revenue issue.
Purchasing the pheasant stamp to hunt ducks would generate more
revenue for the state.

Hunters were told the new source of revenue would help
restore South Dakota to its rightful place as the Pheasant Capital
of the World, or some such nonsense. In reality, all it did was set a
hunter up to fail. As surely as night follows day it was the pheasant
stamp that was missing from the back of the father's Basic License, a
simple oversight that nonetheless landed him in court.

In order to put the matter into its proper context, just two days
prior to the duck season opener at a regional meeting in Sioux Falls,
squeaky-voiced Al Capone stood before fourteen game wardens
and issued a decree: duck hunters missing the pheasant stamp were
hunting ducks without a full and valid license. Al made it clear that
anyone caught hunting ducks without a pheasant stamp was to be
charged as if they were hunting with no license at all.

Al was known for spending as much time figuring out ways to
fire game wardens as he did catching poachers. There was a very real
sense of intimidation that accompanied his pronouncement. Add
the fact that I had only just completed my one-year probationary
period and the stage was set.

So, like the obedient Stormtrooper who said he was only
following orders, the father was issued a ticket for hunting ducks
without a pheasant restoration stamp and summoned into court
in Madison.

CHAPTER THIRTY-ONE

An Undeserved Compliment

That next Thursday at promptly 10 o'clock in the morn-ing, the gentleman hunter from Sioux Falls walked into the courtroom with his wife. Visitors would have surely noticed the gentleman's eye-patch, the same way they would have surely noticed the gentleman's wife when she shuffled into the courtroom with a walker.

When his name was called, the gentleman hunter turned criminal defendant turned and stared into the two eyes of his wife. She stared into his one. Her husband's missing eye had been snatched away decades earlier by a Wehrmacht soldier.

He approached the bench and said meekly, "Guilty, your Honor"; to which the Judge responded, "Fifty dollars and one year loss of hunting privileges!"

The man who would never hunt again stood before the bench, hesitant to take his seat. There was something he wanted to tell the Judge before he left the courtroom. "Your Honor," I heard him say, "the officer who wrote the ticket is one of the finest I've ever met."

CHAPTER THIRTY-TWO

Coca-Cola Diplomacy

A person had to appreciate the constant shenanigans that went on at Wall Lake during my years of service as a game warden in Sioux Falls. I am not exaggerating when I say that gearing up and driving to the lake on yet another summer weekend was like venturing for the first time into unknown territory. Anything was possible and anything happened a lot. In this case, it was my bulletproof vest and a can of ice-cold Coca-Cola that led to this latest anything incident at Wall Lake so long ago.

One of the many things I could have done better as a warden was to stay properly hydrated while on summertime patrol. Nothing dehydrated me faster than wearing a bulletproof vest. It was like sitting in a sauna! Gallons of sweat, it seemed, to the point where I had to become somewhat of a contortionist just to remove my t-shirt. I rarely brought along water or Gatorade to stave off the inevitable cycle of sweating, thirst, and dehydration.

That is why I decided to approach a small group of mostly younger-aged men and women, who were sitting at a picnic table at the Wall Lake boat access area. They had a cooler full of adult beverages and ice-cold sodas. I really wanted an ice-cold soda!

It was with trepidation that I approached the group of revelers to politely ask if I could pay them for a can of soda. "Well, sure!" the big fellow with tattoos and a tank top said. "Help yourself!" So I took a seat alongside my new friends and enjoyed casual conversation accompanied by the most refreshing can of ice-cold soda! It was "Coca-Cola diplomacy" at its finest, and it would pay dividends the very next weekend.

Same time and place the next weekend. I cannot remember the finer details, only that a can came flying out the driver's window of the car. It was a simple case of littering from a motor vehicle that became more complicated when the unidentified driver sped off in a cloud of dust, headed west in the direction of the Bones Ranch Road. His failure to stop resulted in a somewhat mediocre pursuit that lasted all of two miles before the driver stopped and stepped out. I must say that his reaction after stepping from the car was priceless!

Normally a driver would be taken into custody after attempting to elude a law enforcement officer. This was the rare exception. After careful consideration, I ended up charging the driver with only the littering violation and gave him a break on the much more serious charge of attempting to elude.

A breathtakingly hot day, a bulletproof vest, dire thirst and old fashioned Coca-Cola diplomacy were the reasons why the driver chose to stop. What made the incident priceless was when the tattooed man wearing a tank top stood outside his car and said in a plaintive voice, "Dave! I'm sorry, man! If I'd known it was you behind me, I woulda never tried to run!"

CHAPTER THIRTY-THREE

Five Mile Foot Pursuit

Most everyone looks forward to the arrival of spring and the promise of life renewed. Something else pops up each spring with the warmer weather: underage drinking parties. About the only thing that an underage drinking party can promise is death and the enduring pain felt by family and friends.

Death nearly caught up with four young ladies one spring night in Moody County. It started with a party in the country and a traffic stop.

Moody County Sheriff's Deputy Patrick had asked me to ride along that night since he planned to patrol the rural highways near the Moody-Minnehaha County line. He had stopped a young man for speeding and was in the process of writing the ticket when the young man volunteered the location of an underage drinking party. It was being held at a farm about two miles due north from where he had been stopped.

I was standing outside the cruiser (facing west) when my peripheral vision caught the flash of a spinning white light to the northeast. Around and around went the light, only to suddenly disappear. I had turned just in time to see that the spinning white light was a pair of headlights. The inky blackness I was staring at meant the driver had lost control and rolled the car. "Pat! We gotta go, man! Someone just rolled a car!" Off we went, the young man's speeding ticket unfinished.

A car was laying on its side and four young ladies were trying to scramble through a barbed-wire fence. It was actually a relief to see the young ladies running away because running away was a pretty good indicator that none of the young ladies had been seriously injured. Still, the effects of the alcohol and the raging adrenaline could temporarily mask the full extent of their injuries. We first had to catch them to find out.

Once through the fence, they all took off running east through a plowed field. Thus began the "five mile foot pursuit" with me chasing three to the east and Deputy Patrick chasing one to the northeast.

We managed to corral the young ladies, thank goodness! Dell Rapids ambulance was notified and two police officers from Dell Rapids arrived to transport the young ladies to the police station to await the arrival of their parents. One young lady admitted the reason for the accident was her friend saw Deputy Patrick's amber warning lights flashing in the distance and panicked.

How did I manage to corral three fleeing juveniles, with a fairly decent head start, through a plowed field in the darkness of night?

It was my ancestral Irish gift of gab that did the trick. "Hey!" I cried out in my loudest command voice. "I run five miles every day! You might as well stop 'cause I'm gonna catch 'ya!"

CHAPTER THIRTY-FOUR

Blood Smears

I had become emotionally detached, much like a veteri-narian becomes emotionally detached when circumstances require them to euthanize a client's beloved family pet. In my case, it was the assortment of dead wildlife that I had to deal with day after day. It was an endless river of blood and gore that bothered me not at all. Folks who aspire to be a game warden had best not be squeamish when it comes to dealing with dead or dying wildlife, the former often found in some varying degree of decomposition.

Then again, there are exceptions to every rule.

"Five-two-five, five-two-one," I heard the Moody County Sheriff's Dispatcher query over the two-way radio. "A deputy is on a car-deer accident just east of Flandreau, near the Big Sioux River bridge. He'd like you to stop by, if you can." "10-4," I responded, "I'll be there shortly."

A nighttime road-killed deer call was commonplace, just not in the first week of June. Bucks are busy browsing and growing antlers, while does are just beginning to "drop" their fawns and tending to their every need. Deer don't move at night in the spring the way they do in the fall when crop harvest is in full swing and the rut has started. Then it turns into a nightly bloodbath, a spectacle that has to be seen to be believed.

Fifteen minutes later I was at the scene with Deputy Craig, one of my good buddies who had taken the new, fresh-faced game warden under his wing. This time was different. No jocularity.

There, lying in a twisted heap in the beam of my flashlight, were two tiny deer fawn carcasses. They had been blasted, still unborn but fully developed, from their mother's womb upon impact with the car; sliding across ten feet of unforgiving asphalt before coming to a stop. Despite the carnage, I could nonetheless see two tiny chests rising and falling in a tortured rhythm. They were still alive.

It was a decision that was mine to make. So I made a decision, right then and there, knowing it might cost me a friendship. BOOM! BOOM! and the merciful deed was done. Although severely strained at the time, the friendship endured. For that, I will always be grateful.

CHAPTER THIRTY-FIVE

A Frigid August Night

Brant Lake in Lake County is just north of the little town of Chester. Folks familiar with the trail network on the south side of the lake know the trail ends abruptly at the outlet. Before the trail reaches the outlet, it turns ninety degrees to the west. Where it turns is right above a shallow rocky point, which is one of the better areas on the lake to wade and cast for walleye in the spring.

It was the bewitching hour of midnight on a warm and muggy night in August. The angler I called "Dr. Strangelove" was fishing with two of his buddies. It was a routine contact, where it was just me and my wits. Herb, a Lake County Sheriff's Deputy and my one and only backup officer, was busy on a service call.

To their credit the anglers were cooperative. What tripped the alarm was how Dr. Strangelove never made eye contact. Nor did he once turn and face me. He simply pulled his fishing license from a pocket and handed it to me behind his back.

What was it that made me think the man was a wee bit odd? Perhaps it was the fact that the pocket where he kept his fishing license was attached to a full-length winter parka. He even had the hood pulled up, like the good citizen who reported suspicious activity to a sheriff's deputy in the movie Fargo.

No, I did not ask him why!

CHAPTER THIRTY-SIX

A Pregnant Pause

It was another glorious springtime afternoon at Brant Lake. Fishing near the rocky point was a husband and wife from Colman, which is a town in western Moody County. Plus one more! She had a very large "bun in the oven" and was due to give birth in short order!

The bad news is the wife and soon-to-be-mom was fishing without a license. Only her husband had a valid fishing license, which meant the couple could possess only one limit of walleye. Yet the husband was still fishing, despite already having caught a daily limit of walleye that I could see floating belly-up from a stringer that was attached to his waders.

My sudden appearance convinced the prospective parents to call it quits for the day; however, there was still the matter of the no fishing license violation.

Certainly, the thought of writing the wife a ticket for no license crossed my mind, until the soon-to-be-mom did something quite out of the ordinary. She confessed that she habitually fished without a license. "Officer, I deserve a ticket," she said matter-of-factly.

That, as they say, was the deal maker!

A few days later, as I was traveling through Colman, I spotted a familiar beat-up convertible closing the distance behind me. In my rearview mirror was the soon-to-be-mom, riding atop the passenger seat waving her brand spanking new fishing license in the air!

CHAPTER THIRTY-SEVEN

10+2=12

It was the night of high school graduation in Chester, now more than thirty-five years ago. I was patrolling public land on the west side of Brant Lake when I stumbled across a situation somewhat out of the ordinary for a game warden.

It started when I picked up the trail of a white stretch limousine. There, standing through the sunroof, were four happy-go-lucky sorts, each holding a can. I could almost hear the familiar tink! tink! tink! tink! sound as each can landed on the road in front of my truck. Four littering tickets! In an instant, the dazzling red color of a high-intensity strobe light lit up the darkness.

Four heads and torsos popped back into the limousine. Yikes! How was I supposed to identify the four litterbugs from among the many who were surely stuffed inside the limo? That was only the first hurdle. The second hurdle was when the sober professional limousine driver stopped dead center in the road. So had the third hurdle, the Volkswagen "Bug" that was now idling behind me. Ack! They had me wedged in tight, just like a beaver caught in a Hancock trap!

Ten bodies spilled out onto the road from the limousine, then two more from the Bug. HOLY COW! Ten plus two equals twelve young revelers, versus one young game warden who was bound and determined to write four littering tickets. Do the math!

Besides luck, how was a lone game warden going to gain the cooperation of a dozen young people on a remote stretch of a gravel road near the town of Chester? Certainly not by acting like a bully, the way oathbreakers do as a matter of routine.

No, being a bully was out of the question. A much better option was to be polite and professional because it was pretty much the only option that had any chance of success.

Ask any experienced officer what happens to the volatility level of a young person who is under ANY level of influence from alcohol. Now, ask the same officer what happens when there is more than one young person under the influence of alcohol and they surround a young game warden on a remote stretch of gravel road near Chester? I would bet there are plenty of officers who would rather pick peaches for a living.

Being polite and professional was a strategy but it was still only a strategy. What remained was an answer to the "now what" question, as in "now what do I do?" My answer was "the correct application of officer discretion!"

"Say, I'm not here to ruin your night," I began to explain to the vast crowd of adolescents. "That's the last thing I want to do. But I hope you all understand that the littering tickets are non-negotiable. Littering is the reason you're talking to a game warden right now. The good news is that's all I'm interested in. Whatever else might be going on inside the limo stays inside the limo. Understood?"

There was something else, something I was overlooking that would seal the deal on their cooperation. How in the world did I forget?

"Guys, just so you know, there are two state troopers just up the road on Highway 34. They can be here right quick, and I'm pretty sure you know what that means!"

It took forty minutes to write the tickets and everyone remained on their best behavior. Thank goodness for the South Dakota Highway Patrol!

This is how officer safety works, by doing what is appropriate and necessary to win hearts and minds when the option of assembling a mini-platoon of backup officers is out of the question. Will oathbreakers pay attention?

By the way, there were no state troopers just up the road. There was nothing just up the road. I had been on my own from the start.

CHAPTER THIRTY-EIGHT

Uncle Bob

I encountered Uncle Bob and three of his family mem-bers on Brant Lake during a Fourth of July boating safety patrol. All four were fishing for walleye and had had fair success. Three of the four began searching for their fishing licenses but I kindly waved them off. Instead, I asked if they could introduce me to the gentleman sitting in the back of the boat, the one with a fishing pole held fast by a withered forearm.

Uncle Bob had been an American "Doughboy", having served in France during WWI. Whether the family members mentioned a particular battle or branch of service are details that I simply cannot recall. They shared that Bob's withered forearm was the consequence of his service. Uncle Bob managed to look me in the eye and smile, which the family members said was his unique way of saying hi.

Yet, there was still a very real sense of uneasiness among the family members, beyond the normal amount that manifested whenever I made a surprise appearance. So I gave them a wink, letting them know that everything would be fine; that I knew Uncle Bob did not have a fishing license, and that over my dead body would I ask to see the fishing license of an elderly American war hero who was clearly on his last outdoor adventure.

CHAPTER THIRTY-NINE

Twenty Years in Twenty Minutes

In mid-November, 1983, in response to a hunting tres-pass complaint in southeastern Moody County, I happened across two deer poachers from Dell Rapids. Kevin had two freshly-killed deer laying in the bed of his pickup truck, deer that he and a hunting companion had killed with bow and arrow but failed to tag. I seized both deer and the men's unused archery tags and cited the poachers into court in Flandreau.

Within the week both men were standing before the Judge, each facing a charge of illegal transportation and possession of deer. They both pled guilty and were ordered to pay a $50 fine and spend three days in jail, with the jail time suspended upon successful completion of probation. But the part of the sentence that stung the most was when the Judge revoked their hunting privileges for one year.

It was the first time I had stirred up the hornet's nest of hardcore poachers from Dell Rapids, a small group of men whom I'd been duly warned about shortly after I moved to Flandreau. Their favorite area was four square miles of contiguous territory along the

Big Sioux River in the southcentral part of the county. It was theirs for the taking. Even the farmers looked the other way out of fear of retaliation.

Fast forward twenty years. I was now the Assistant Chief Game Warden living in Pierre, patrolling a portion of southeastern Lake County during the East River Deer Season. I was traveling west on a gravel road when I popped over a hill in time to see something odd, even for a game warden with twenty years on the job.

There, on the road ahead of me traveling in the same direction, was a pickup truck. Just in front of the pickup was a hunting dog feverishly working the road ditches. Back and forth the dog ran, darting into and out of one ditch, then the other, as the mysterious man behind the wheel crept forward. With the barrel of his shotgun sticking out the window.

With few exceptions, it was illegal to allow a firearm to protrude from a motor vehicle while on a public road; and, even if the driver had a valid disabled hunter permit to shoot from a motor vehicle - which he did not, coincidently - he was still required to come to a complete stop before firing.

Several minutes went by before I realized the futility of waiting for a rooster to haphazardly flush from a road ditch in heavily-farmed Lake County. So I decided to stop the truck and have a little chat with the two men inside.

It was Kevin from Dell Rapids behind the wheel. I thought, if only his dog had flushed a rooster and Kevin had blasted at it from the truck, he would pay another fine and lose his hunting privileges for another year! Everything changed the instant Kevin stepped from the truck.

Recall that the only Kevin I knew for twenty years was a hardcore poacher. He had not changed his ways, obviously. He had earned the ticket I was about to write for gun protrusion. So why, after twenty minutes of sitting and chatting with Kevin inside my truck, was the ticket form still untouched?

Our shared humanity was the reason behind my decision to issue Kevin only a written warning; the reason why I shook Kevin's hand and wished him all the best before we parted ways. My former adversary was still recovering from the many life-threatening injuries he sustained after surviving a near-fatal car accident - the accident that killed his girlfriend.

CHAPTER FORTY

A Grimm Fairy Tale

As hardcore poachers go, Kevin was a minor league player who aspired to play in the big leagues. That was not the case with the two 'Grimm' brothers from Dell Rapids. Those boys played in the big leagues, only instead of bringing a baseball glove they brought loaded weapons and a burning hatred for game wardens.

It was inevitable that our paths would cross. They did, on an isolated stretch of road in the northernmost part of Moody County on the second day of the 1983 East River Deer Season. At the time of our chance encounter, I had been a game warden for three months.

Welcome to Flandreau.

In the world of wildlife law enforcement, there are essentially two types of poaching reports that will sooner or later make their way to the local game warden: "active" and "latent". An "active" report involves a poacher who committed a specific wildlife-related crime only recently, which then lends itself to the warden opening a full-blown criminal investigation.

A "latent" report, on the other hand, is comprised mainly of an abundance of rumors, personal opinions, and logical inferences. Together, they reveal an unmistakable pattern - the who, what, where, when, and how - of chronic poaching activity. Unlike an active report, however, a latent poaching report lacks sufficient details to open a criminal investigation. Latent reports are valuable nonetheless, as they help the warden focus and prioritize his patrol efforts.

There is an implicit understanding between a seasoned poacher, one whose poaching activity falls into the latent category, and the local game warden. More to the point, it is the same kind of mercurial relationship that exists between two boxers as they circle one another in the ring. They may not make direct eye contact, but they know not to turn their back to the opponent.

As much as I heard about the Grimm brothers, it is surprising that I never received an active poaching report. This meant the Grimm brothers were either highly-skilled poachers who refrained from bragging or the locals were simply too afraid to turn them in.

Since their reputation as poachers was widespread, my guess is that the locals remained unconvinced that it would be a good idea to report the Grimm brothers. It was not worth the expense of replacing four flat tires or finding out that the gas in the gas tank had been enriched with high fructose corn syrup.

Being a young game warden who worked far too many hours, it was inevitable that I would develop bone-deep fatigue from lack of sleep. Thus it was in a state of abject physical and mental exhaustion that I left Flandreau early that Sunday morning, way back in 1983.

My truck seemed to be on autopilot as I turned west onto the Ward-Nunda Road, destined for a particular gravel road that would take me north to the Moody-Brookings County line. My intent was to maintain enforcement pressure on the area where I had caught four deer poachers the previous morning.

There was a snow-filled cornfield that blocked my view to the west as I neared the county line. The field, like so many others, was a casualty of the winter of '83-'84, the worst winter I worked as a game warden. But the worst of the winter weather was still a month away, something I was unaware of as I negotiated the two-wheel-drive pickup through a left turn on the county line.

There, 100 yards due west, sat a jacked-up pickup truck with three men milling about...all staring in my direction.

CHAPTER FORTY-ONE

He's in the Basement

"Say, I'm headed over to North Spring Avenue to serve a bench warrant on a guy for failing to appear on a fishing license case," I said to Al Capone, "and I was wondering if you'd like to come along?"

It turned out to be a very fortuitous request.

During my time in Sioux Falls, the Minnehaha County Sheriff's Office averaged around 10,000 unserved arrest warrants. In relative terms, my case-related warrants were few, far, and unlikely to be served unless I was willing to serve the warrants myself.

There is more to the story than just serving an arrest warrant on a no-show scofflaw. As a game warden, I had to work hard to catch poachers, at least in comparison to other types of crime. Unlike a traffic cop who benefits from a machine telling them when someone is breaking the law, I had to go out and make cases on my own. It made no sense to go through the work, only to have a poacher escape justice by thumbing their nose at the judicial system.

There was yet another reason why I went after no-show scofflaws with such fervor. If left unserved, a misdemeanor warrant was going to disappear from the system after two years.

It was a combination of hard work; judicial insolence; the issuance of a warrant; the disappearance of a warrant; and the need to hold poachers accountable that drove my determination to find the scofflaws. This is why Al and I were headed to North Spring Avenue in central Sioux Falls to serve a bench warrant on a scofflaw named 'Trevor'.

Knock-knock and the front door slowly opened. Standing on the opposite side of the screen door was an older gentlewoman, who listened to our explanation and kindly invited us into her modest but well-kept home.

If one were to stand just outside and look in, what they would see is a front door that opened in and to the right, which then led into the living room. At the far end of the living room, on the left, was the entry into the kitchen. At the far end of the living room, on the right, was the door to the basement.

"Ma'am, we'd really like to speak with Trevor. We understand that he's been staying at this address," I explained quietly. "He was supposed to appear in court for fishing without a license, but he probably just forgot."

We learned Trevor was her grandson. Now, before anyone conjures up an image of Trevor as some snot-nosed kid eating a peanut butter and jelly sandwich, he was nothing of the sort. While Trevor may have liked to eat a peanut butter and jelly sandwich with a snotty nose, he was no kid. Trevor was a strapping, twenty-something brute with a rather lengthy criminal record.

As hazardous as it was to attempt to arrest someone like Trevor, what made the matter such a distraction was the fact that we were standing inside the home of an elderly widow. As if that were not disconcerting enough, because I was a game warden, very few saw me as a "real" law enforcement officer.

That condescending attitude went so far as to permeate the thinking of other law enforcement officers. For instance, the female police officer from Sioux Falls who, upon seeing me escort a prisoner into the jail's intake area, laughed out loud and said, "You're just a game warden! Since when do you bring people to jail?"

Infamous words spoken by a member of the "real" law enforcement profession, the one whose members have to summon countless backup officers before approaching a kid with a Red Ryder BB gun.

Now parlay that type of thinking to the level of the governor and state legislature, neither of whom cared much for game wardens, and it should be clear why performing law enforcement kept me on tenterhooks. Like the Molly Hatchet song with the same name, attempting to make an arrest in the home of an elderly widow was "flirting with disaster".

After making small talk and answering her questions, I asked Trevor's grandmother if she would please tell us where to find Trevor. "He's in the basement," she said without hesitation.

We had no reason to believe Trevor's grandmother would lie. So Al and I walked over to the basement door, confident that Trevor was hiding somewhere in the inky blackness below. Al stood a few feet behind me looking over my shoulder, while I stood at the top of the stairs and called out Trevor's name.

Somewhere hiding in the tiny home was Trevor. We had no idea just how close he was.

CHAPTER FORTY-TWO

A Grimm Fifty Miles

It was the Grimm brothers and a friend milling about the back end of the truck when I pulled up. My attention was focused not so much on the men at the time, but on the steam rising in waves from the bed of the pickup. A fresh kill, no doubt.

I had only met the Grimm brothers the day before when they stopped to exchange "pleasantries" just south of where we were now parked. Their jacked-up 4x4 pickup dwarfed my tiny, two-wheel-drive work truck. As a matter of fact, the truck sat so high that I had to poke my head out the window and crane my neck just to carry on a conversation. Even then, I spent most of the conversation talking to the door handle.

From my perspective, it was as if the brothers were riding a Harley-Davidson "knucklehead" motorcycle with dual leather saddlebags on the back, whereas I was riding a Big Wheel "Scorcher" tricycle with pink sparkle scooter streamers tied to the handlebars.

It was a freshly killed "button buck" whitetail in the bed of the truck. Although the deer appeared to be properly tagged, I had to scramble up and over the tailgate to read the fine print on the tag. No sooner had I looked at the tag that I knew the deer had been poached.

How I knew the deer had been poached was because it was 8:30 in the morning, the ambient air temperature was 20 °F, the deer was warm to the touch, and because of the steam that arose from the gutted carcass.

There was also the matter of the deer tag, the one that had the name and address of the friend - along with "Kingsbury County" - printed across the top. Kingsbury County was at least 50 miles from where the four of us were standing.

As I watched the Grimm brothers drive away that frigid and overcast morning, I could not help but ask myself what just happened? For goodness sakes, I had both Grimm brothers and their friend dead to rights, with charges that would have carried hefty fines and the loss of hunting privileges for a year. Yet, there they went, with the deer still in the bed of the truck after having been caught red-handed by the new Moody County Game Warden. How they must have laughed all the way back to Dell Rapids, and rightfully so.

They had gotten off scot-free because I was too new to know how to perform a proper field interview and too tired to remember to take a temperature reading of a hindquarter.

That was my first, and last, chance to catch the Grimm brothers. Because of my incompetence, the Grimm brothers continued to poach and wildlife continued to die.

CHAPTER FORTY-THREE

Where's Trevor

We were having no luck trying to coax Trevor from the basement. "Trevor," I called out one last time, "it's only a fishing license ticket. There's no reason for you to put your grandmother through this, and in her home of all places!"

We heard a distinctly masculine voice behind us say, "Yeah, you're right." We turned and saw Trevor. He had been hiding behind the front door the entire time.

CHAPTER FORTY-FOUR

Two Clans in One Hour

The Conclusion to the Last Chapter of
"The Forgotten Lawmen Part 5"

He smashed his sledgehammer-sized fists against the steering wheel of the pickup and yelled, "WE RAISE THESE [EXPLETIVE] PHEASANTS! FISH AND GAME DON'T RAISE A [EXPLETIVE] BIRD! THERE WOULDN'T BE A [EXPLETIVE] PHEASANT IF NOT FOR US FARMERS!"

Now fully enraged, the monstrous man behind the wheel made a quick grab for the door handle and started to open the door. I closed the door before he could step out, sealing him inside the cab by pushing down on the lock knob at the top of the door. It worked!

I saw movement to my right and turned instinctively. There, atop the bed rail, was first one, then two distinctly styled hunting boots. With two boots came six more, which meant the boys were about to come over the side. How did this happen? What had I done wrong? THINK! What should I do? THINK FASTER!

It had started earlier when I ran headlong into the T. Clan hunting rooster pheasants on a federal "Waterfowl Production Area", lands that are open to the public for hunting and other outdoor pursuits. Acting together, the ten or so men in the hunting party were a well-oiled killing machine. Any pheasant that had the misfortune of flushing within shotgun range was down to its last two seconds on earth.

As I approached, one of the hunting dogs jumped up and smeared the front of my uniform pants with muddy paw prints. That was followed by the same hunting dog walking across the clipboard that I had laid on the ground. "Good dog!" I heard amongst a chorus of dark and hearty laughter. So I was not all that surprised when my departure was met with many wishes for a long and happy life.

To the east a few miles were ten hunters affiliated with the W. Clan. Three hunters stood on the road acting as "blockers", while the remaining seven walked a picked cornfield towards the road. They were hoping to push pheasants within gun range of the blockers, all of which was perfectly legal in South Dakota at the time.

A deer sprang from its bed in front of the line of walkers! Dark and lightning fast, the deer ran toward the road and the line of blockers. One effortless leap and the doe was over the barbed wire fence and up onto the road! The blocker closest to me shouldered his shotgun...and pointed it at the fast-moving deer.

Luckily he held off shooting the deer, considering there was a game warden watching just a short distance to the north. Then it dawned on me that the hunter knew I was a game warden and that he was being a showman and wise-guy. Funny! It took some nerve to do that right in front of a game warden. Was this a precursor of things to come?

The walkers finally met up with the blockers and the two groups stood and mingled on the road. First was the showman and wise-guy, now this. What I had noticed was one of the blockers pass their shotgun to one of the walkers and scoot inside a white pickup truck. Once inside, the driver and now-weaponless hunter sped off to the south.

Fifteen minutes later I was standing outside the driver's door of the white pickup, dealing with an enraged farmer and his four grown sons. At the time, I was too naive not to realize that others get to vote on the appropriateness of an officer's behavior. It was while I was interviewing the hunter who fled that I had rolled my eyes and scoffed.

It was MY fault for the mess, which made it MY mess to clean up. The only way to clean up the mess was to do something very few police officers seem willing to do. I said I was sorry.

Yes, the officer had reasonable suspicion to believe that a burglary had been committed. Stopping, detaining, and identifying the driver and passenger would be lawful under a Terry Stop.

There is a <u>3-step process</u> for determining if reasonable suspicion to stop and detain exists:

Step 1: Can the officer ARTICULATE facts and circumstances that allow him to identify a specific crime or crimes that he believes has occurred, is occurring, or is about to occur? In this example, the facts and circumstances are:

1. 2:20 am
2. Store is CLOSED
3. A car is parked on the far side of the convenience store
4. No car(s) are parked in a normal fashion in front of the convenience store
5. Two quick flashes of light from a vehicle that appear to be aimed at the mom and pop store
6. Flashes appear to be a signal to someone inside the store
7. Several minutes later the headlights come on
8. The vehicle crosses the street and pulls in front of the mom and pop store

9. Seconds later a shadowy figure runs from the store and jumps into the car, which quickly drives off

Has a specific crime been identified by the officer with these known facts? <u>YES</u>! What crime? <u>BURGLARY</u>!

Step 2: Is the SOURCE of the information deemed RELIABLE? <u>YES</u>! It is from the personal observations of a law enforcement officer who is automatically deemed reliable.

Step 3: Has the officer CORROBORATED sufficient information from a reliable source to make the investigative detention? <u>YES</u>! HOW? The officer puts all of the facts together UNDER THE TOTALITY OF THE CIRCUMSTANCES (which is the judicial test for reasonable suspicion) and corroborates that what he has observed is, in fact, a burglary. What were the burglars willing to risk going to prison for? Beer.

It should be noted that the officer who apprehended the burglars eventually retired after more than twenty years of service in law enforcement. Rumor has it that the old, gray-haired former officer writes books about his many adventures, although the jury is still out on whether the stories are all that entertaining.

FOR FREEDOM,
TROY, MAINE
FEBRUARY 2019 - JUNE 2020